I CHOOSE THE SKY

A SCRIPTURAL DEVOTION FOR WOMEN

BY EMILY WILSON

○ LIFE TEEN

Authored by Emily Wilson

Designed by Gracie Wilson, Casey Olson

Copy editing by Rachel Peñate, Joel Stepanek

A special thanks to all those who have contributed to this resource in its original form.

Published by Life Teen, Inc.
2222 S. Dobson Rd. Suite 601
Mesa, AZ 85202
LifeTeen.com

Printed in the United States of America. Printed on acid-free paper.

ALL MY LOVE
AND GRATITUDE TO
WILSON WORLD,
MY CHEERFUL DANIËL,
AND MRS. NICK.

TABLE OF CONTENTS

FOREWORD

By Mark Hart

My wife loves romantic comedies... which means, quite simply, that I now love romantic comedies. When I invite her to watch sci-fi or action movies her response is often the same, "I just don't get into them. They're not realistic. I don't care about the characters." Of course, a universe where Ryan Gosling is unlucky at love is *supremely* realistic... but I digress. Put simply, for my wife to care about a movie or any story, she has to care about the characters within it. She has to "connect" with them far more than I do, as a man.

Now, this is not to be stereotypical or to overly-generalize genders. I know plenty of women who love a good action movie and plenty of guys who genuinely enjoy romantic comedies (or so they claim). What it does reveal, I believe, is how beautifully and wonderfully made both genders are, yet, how differently men and women process things.

The Bible sets the stage on our gender complementarity right out of the gate, actually. We're not even through the first chapter of Genesis when we see that God created male and female equal, but quite different. While both man and woman were made in God's image and likeness, and both are the result of His great love (1 John 4:8, 19), they are unique, distinct, and different in their origin.

I

Go back to the first words of Genesis and watch as the Father creates. Every level of creation brought with it an increased artistry and complexity. We move from darkness to light, to sea and land and sky, to animals to man and then, finally, to woman.

God outdid Himself when he created the man's counterpart. God has style. I mean, c'mon. Breathing light into darkness is epic. Forming and distinguishing the sky from the stars, stellar, but creating a creature with not only a body but also a soul... capable of co-creating and bringing life? That is a masterpiece. Assuredly, as important and great as the creation of the man was, if the man is the "crown" of creation, than the woman is the crown jewel of it.

Now, you might be thinking, "This is a book, written by a woman, for women, about Biblical women... so why is a man writing the foreword?" Because women are the most glorious of God's creation, valuable beyond compare and beautiful beyond measure. This reality of the worth and dignity of women has been sadly denied, reduced and misplaced in modern culture and it is time to regain our proper perspective. Speaking as a husband and father to three beautiful daughters, I celebrate the glory that is woman and thank God, daily, for the gift that you are to the world. I'm writing this because not only does this author, Emily, continually impress me with her ministry and amaze me in her insights, but this book deepened my own appreciation for the heroic women you'll read more about and further grew my respect and admiration for the female gender, in general!

If a man were to say "woman is a great mystery" in today's culture, sadly, most would take it as a punch line to a joke... an offhanded and snarky "male" comment meant to in some way condescend or demoralize their far fair-er female counterpart. Properly understood, however, in a spirit of reverence, awe, and gratitude, proclaiming that woman is "a great mystery" is, actually, one of the highest compliments to be paid. Woman is a mystery – glorious and gorgeous and estimable – a mystery to be cherished and to behold. While man was fashioned from the earth, from the external; woman was fashioned from the rib – she comes from the internal. The woman is by nature more naturally disposed to the interior movements of her heart, to deep contemplation, to earlier emotional maturity, and to greater emotional presence. There is an obvious beauty and majesty to women: Created with something timeless and innate and glorious - a maternal instinct as some call it. God breathes this internal GPS into every woman, regardless of her vocation, a spiritual roadmap through which she loves in deep and selfless ways.

While some people might point to Sacred Scripture as antiquated or sexist, God reveals time and time again His great admiration for women. The highest and greatest saint in the entire Communion of Saints is a woman. The Blessed Virgin Mary is the only person (outside of the Holy Trinity) to be present at the three most important events in the history of the world: the Nativity, the Triduum, and Pentecost. The longest recorded dialogue with Jesus in the gospels occurred between Him and the Samaritan woman at the well. The first witness to the Resurrection, you ask? A female disciple. I could go on but I'll let the chapters that follow do that, instead.

You are blessed to have a guide on this devotional journey like Emily. She is a woman after Mary's own heart – who has taken these timeless stories and characters into her own heart. She's stared deeply into their eyes and peered into their souls and on the pages that follow she'll invite you to do the same. To ask, "What made these people live and act and respond as they did? How did the love and grace of God impel and propel them forward to greater virtue?"

Just as our Mother Mary "kept and pondered all these things in her heart" (Luke 2:19), you will be invited to follow in her immaculate footsteps, doing just that, yourself.

Take your time reading and praying through this book. Pause, frequently, to revisit these stories on the pages of your own Bible. Take time during each chapter to speak to your Father or, better yet, to allow Him to speak to you. Share with your friends and sisters in Christ the passages that most strike you, the verses that most comfort you, or the lines that most convict

you. In doing so, you will soon find this work to be more of a retreat than a resource, more a journey than just a walk. As I've learned from my wife's preference in movies, "connecting" with the characters really does make me more invested in the story.

One last thought: in His perfect wisdom, God made you a woman. He knit you in your mother's womb (Psalm 139) and fashioned you a beauty for all to behold (Proverbs 31). God's plan for you is intimately tied to His design in you. Your ultimate joy, vocation, and peace will be found not by obsessing about the creation (your body, life, future) but, rather, by getting to know better your Creator and Father. With every chapter, enter into this love story from the Father to His daughters, and hear Him speak of your inestimable worth and immense beauty.

This father is thankful for this book to pass along to my own daughters... for there is a reason God shared these stories with us so many centuries ago, and a reason we keep on telling them. Thank you for sharing the gift of your femininity with a world so desperately in need of it. May our Mother Mary kneel beside you as you pray the pages to come.

INTRODUCTION

There are almost 200 named women in the Bible, and many more without names.

This work is about seventeen of them.

They are seventeen women whose lives were woven into the tapestry of the greatest book ever written - the Bible, the very Word of God.

They are women who are easy to overlook if you are not paying attention in a book filled with many hundreds of men - they can be easily forgotten and are often ignored completely. Many of them lived thousands of years ago - but the witness that these women made to a life in Christ cannot be swept aside. Their stories are relevant. Their stories matter. Their encounters with Christ have volumes to teach us.

I decided to bring their stories to life because these women have shown me how to live.

In this book, we will journey with these women. We will learn from their actions and their virtues and their personal encounters with Jesus Christ. Their stories are vast wells of truth and knowledge about who God is and who He created us to be as women. We will walk with women who lived lives of hardship and struggle and had momentous personal encounters with Jesus in his three years of ministry. We will watch their

selflessness. We will bask in their bravery. We will be empowered by their decision to rise at the call of Christ. We will learn about brazen evangelization and having a heart of hospitality and giving until it hurts. We will think about our priorities and God's pursuit of our messy hearts, and just how crucial it is to be a woman who is kind. We will reflect on loyalty and the power in our voices and how God's mercy covers every breath of our existence.

As I have journeyed with these women, I have come to understand more deeply what it means to choose God above all things. In our broken world, focusing on sorrow, suffering, negativity, and heartbreak is an effortless choice - but the life God has planned for each of us is filled with astounding joy and love - and the challenge comes in choosing to see that joy and love. Choosing the sky is about deciding to look up and out - from ourselves and our own troubles - to see Christ in the everyday and Christ alive in the person before us. Choosing the sky is all about recognizing the beauty, love, and joy overflowing from the heart of God in this world and in our lives. It is about choosing compassion over selfishness, hope over fear, a cheerful heart over a morose heart, and choosing to hold fast to faith in every season of life. These women have shown me how to do just this.

Jesus encountered a number of these women in person, and looked on them with an incredible and astonishing love. The words He shares with them will take your breath away the moment you realize He wants to look at you - just as He looked at them - and speak those same words to your heart. *Go in peace. Be healed of your affliction. Weep no more. Your faith has saved you. You are set free.*

God wants to speak to you through these women. I invite you to open yourself to Him as you walk with these stories of our sisters in Christ who have been claimed by our loving, powerful, and merciful God for His own. Let their stories move you - give their stories the power to change your life - allow room in your heart for the lessons that can make us better, stronger, and more courageous daughters of God.

The love of God our Father covers each and every one of us, every day of our lives.

Let His love cover you as His daughter, while you journey through these pages.

Let His love wash over you as His own.

These women, and you and I - we are all His daughters, living in the glorious light of His Resurrection. We are women who choose the sky.

OUR GOD OF COMPASSION

THE WIDOW AT NAIN

Soon afterwards he went to a town called Nain, and his disciples and a large crowd went with him. As he approached the gate of the town, a man who had died was being carried out. He was his mother's only son, and she was a widow; and with her was a large crowd from the town. When the Lord saw her, he had compassion for her and said to her, "Do not weep." Then he came forward and touched the bier, and the bearers stood still. And he said, "Young man, I say to you, rise!" The dead man sat up and began to speak, and Jesus gave him to his mother. Fear seized all of them; and they glorified God, saying, "A great prophet has risen among us!" and "God has looked favorably on his people!" This word about him spread throughout Judea and all the surrounding country.

--Luke 7: 11-17

When I was eighteen years old, I set foot onto the second-biggest university in the United States. There were 65,000 students; we were our own city. At this university I was registered under my name, but once classes began my name was no longer necessary. I was a number: #1200045547. I wrote it on all my exams - my name was not even needed on assignments or tests. I sat in stadium-seating classrooms of 300 or more students. I did not know my professors. I was just another person among the masses, just another face in the crowd.

Do you ever feel as though God must have so many people to care for, with troubles so much bigger than yours, that you must be very far down on His list? I wonder if the widow at Nain ever felt this way. At the moment we meet her in Scripture, this woman's future looks incredibly lonely.

Her husband died, leaving her a widow, and she was left with her one son. During this time, upon his father's death, her son would have been the main caretaker of his mother and the home. In an unfortunate circumstance, her son - her only protector, provider, and companion - dies as well. You can imagine the excruciating grief she felt at the reality of having to live alone with no family to care for her in her progressing age. She walked along in this procession with a heart broken beyond measure.

When Jesus, the Savior of the world, looks upon this crowd of people, He does not see a crowd. He sees her. *Our God is a God of intimacy.* In our culture, intimacy has become synonymous with sexual experiences, but when we refer to intimacy with God, we use the word by its true definition - the existence of closeness between two beings. God desires this close, personal relationship with each of us. As Jesus stands witnessing the procession for the widow's son, He knows the personal needs, sorrows, and joys of each person in the crowd with this woman. He knows the heart of each person He has ever brought into existence. In approaching the widow, Jesus shows us with great clarity that none of us is or will ever be a number or a face in the crowd to Him. You are not just another person in the world - you are His daughter, precious and beautiful in His sight. The prayers you speak to God the Father are not simply added to His list of things to attend to. When you attend Mass on Sunday, you are not just a speck in the congregation to the Lord. Your presence in His house is individually recognized and rejoiced in by the Heavenly Father. Christ cares for each of us in the deepest, most personal way imaginable.

It is an astonishing truth which can take your breath away when you really reflect on it...

You are of utmost importance to the God of the universe because you are His creation.

He fashioned you with greatest attention, with deep love and a divine purpose in the masterpiece of the world He has composed with supreme care. He gave life to the world, the oceans, the stars and trees and mountains. God breathed life into you. *Sister, your life is significant.*

As you will find with many of the women in this book, the widow at Nain is in serious pain. However, in a stark contrast to the hemorrhaging woman and the sinful woman, the widow at Nain does not go to find Jesus. She does not seek Him. He comes to meet her exactly where she is.

She is broken-hearted. Sorrowful. Lonely. And Jesus Christ finds her right in the middle of it all.

He approaches her - in the storm of this unexplainable ache, in the midst of burying her only child - and He meets her with compassion. He stops for a woman without a name. His heart, both human and divine, is deeply moved for her.

When we open our hearts to intimacy with our Creator in the midst of suffering, we can find profound comfort that we will never find in earthly things.

Christ knows your suffering. He holds the sun and the stars at the same time that He holds your needs and sorrows. He wants to reveal His presence in your life, hold your face in his hands and speak peace, "Weep no more." *He wants to meet you right where you are.*

And in His great power and omnipotence, you are always number one on the list. It is a truth that extends past our comprehension, but is a truth that stands for each one of us. There is no person with problems, struggles, or pain more important to God than yours.

He knows you. He loves you. He is keeping your heart beating and keeping the earth in motion all at the same time. What reality will ever be more spectacular than this?

PRAYER

Lord, I know you are a God of intimacy and that you have counted every hair on my head (Matthew 10:30). When I feel as heartbroken, discouraged, and lonely as the widow at Nain, help me to know and remember that you care deeply about my pain and my struggles and you are present to meet me in them. In the moments where I cannot fathom just how important I am to you - help me to remember that you fashioned the oceans and the sky and fashioned me with your very own hand, and that you never stop thinking of me for one second. Amen.

REFLECTION

- Has it ever seemed as though you've been forgotten or as though you were just another face in the crowd? Maybe in your family, in your group of friends, or at your school? How did that make you feel?

- What has the widow's experience with Jesus taught you about your importance to your Creator?

PRIORITY
NUMBER ONE

MARY AND MARTHA

Now as they went on their way, he entered a certain village, where a woman named Martha welcomed him into her home. She had a sister named Mary, who sat at the Lord's feet and listened to what he was saying. But Martha was distracted by her many tasks; so she came to him and asked, "Lord, do you not care that my sister has left me to do all the work by myself? Tell her then to help me." But the Lord answered her, "Martha, Martha, you are worried and distracted by many things; there is need of only one thing. Mary has chosen the better part, which will not be taken away from her."

--Luke 10: 38-42

There has never been a time in the history of the universe when people were more "busy" than we are today. We hear it all the time:

"I'm sorry, I can't. I'm too busy."

"I was so busy I forgot."

"There's just too much to do and not enough hours in the day."

I am busy. Busy working. Busy with studying and school. Busy with my friends. Busy with sports and activities. Busy trying to find a boyfriend. Busy with applying to college or grad school. Busy babysitting. Busy planning my life. Busy exercising. Busy scanning social media. Busy trying to find a job. Busy checking things off my to-do list.

Where on Earth does a relationship with Jesus Christ fit into all this busyness?

It should fit right in at number one. There is, after all, need of only one thing. Christ says it in plain words... there is need of one thing and Mary has chosen it. The best part. She has chosen to sit and spend time with the Lord and listen to Him speak His words of truth and life into her heart.

Imagine this... the Lord is in your neighborhood and He stops by your home. You have a great dinner and then He goes with everyone in the living room to spend some time with them. Can you imagine saying to him, "Sorry, Lord, can't listen now. I'm too busy scanning my news feeds."

Never! The news feeds can *wait!* The Lord is *speaking* in your living room!

It is synonymous with those who refused a place for Joseph and Mary as she prepared to give birth to the Savior of the world. Nobody wanted to make space for Him...they knocked on door after door, and *everyone's houses and lives were full.*

This is a sad representation of what our lives look like all too often. Our Lord wants us to come to Mass, or to Eucharistic Adoration, or to stop by church even for a couple of moments to spend time with Him. If we cannot do that, He wants us to simply set aside some time for daily prayer at home to be in relationship with Him. And all too often we say, *"Lord, I've got things to do. Sorry...can't listen now."*

Certainly, there is homework to be done. There are exams to study for and everyone needs time to hang out with friends. There are to-do lists

to check off in every person's life. But as we go through this list we let our relationship with Jesus fall to second place, then fifth, then tenth, then no place at all. Sometimes we decide we are just too busy to pray.

When we are too busy to pray, that is a clear indication that things are out of order.

During high school, I did not pray every day. I went to Mass every Sunday and prayed on occasion during the week. God was often times an afterthought. When I got to college, I went through some immense challenges and began to pray every day by going to the daily Mass held on campus. The chapel was the only place I felt peace in the midst of a challenging workload and extremely disheartening troubles with friends. My life changed completely, for the better, in many ways, when I committed to going to Mass for 30 minutes every day. I had not even realized what I was missing until a few weeks into my commitment, but once I experienced the peace of a steady prayer life, I began to feel a great sense of fulfillment in my heart. A steady prayer life requires worthwhile discipline; there is no good prayer life based on laziness or convenience. I decided that 30 minutes, in the grand scheme of each day, was not much time at all to give, and the benefits of making this a part of my every day were many.

I began to feel great peace, and I began to look forward to that time I got to spend with God. That decision to dedicate myself to daily prayer has carried from that time forward. It expanded into a desire to read Scripture, and I began by reading five minutes a day in a Gospel and reflecting on what I read. The more I read God's Word, the more I wanted to be immersed in it. That became an important part of my walk with God as well - reading about Jesus' life helped me get to know Him in a more intimate way.

My relationship with God and my prayer life have never been perfect - there are times when I do become like Martha - seemingly too busy for God or Mass or prayer in any form. But when we set aside time to do these things and get into a rhythm and discipline of daily prayer, we become more steady, more peaceful, more patient and slow to anger, and easier to get along with. We become more in tune with the ways we sin against God. We become much, much more joyful. Everyone around us is looking for happiness and believes there is some formula to gaining happiness in life; everyone has an opinion on what will really make people happy. I will let you in on a secret that I have found to be true time and time again... the happiest, most patient and loving people I know spend time in prayer every single day. Have you ever met one of those religious sisters just beaming

with an astounding peace and joy? Sisters spend more time in prayer than most everybody you will ever meet.

One of the most common excuses we can make about spending time with the Lord is that He is *always* around. We fall into not praying because we know...in six weeks, in a few months, in a year, God will still be there. Can you imagine a friendship where you never called, except for when you felt like it or needed something? That wouldn't really be a friendship, or a relationship, at all. There would be no way for you to continue to grow, to continue to get to know one another and become better friends if those were the only occasions that you would contact them, and truly... you wouldn't really know each other. Our relationship with God is the same way - He is always there, but how are we to ever grow with Him if we rarely spend time with Him because we know He is ever-present? If we only call on God when we need something or want to pray for someone we know who is in great need, we never give ourselves the opportunity to get to know God. *Unwrapping the gift of knowing God is one of the most wonderful adventures of this earthly life.*

When we walk with God, we are also better able to see what things should be priorities in our lives. Do you need to join that extra club, play that extra sport, take that extra class all in the name of having a more impressive résumé for college or graduate school? What if you worked hard, did a reasonable amount of extracurricular activities, and trusted that God would make a way for you to get to the place He planned for you to go? Walk with God and what should be priorities in your life will become apparent. You may come to see that time with family is precious - that spending every single day of summer vacation with friends may become every other day when you think of how much your mom or dad or siblings would love to spend some time with you. You may come to see that you actually do have an hour every weekend to go to Mass - because each one of us always will, this I promise you. You and I will always have an hour on the weekends to dedicate to our loving and generous God and receive His body into the tabernacle of our hearts. *There is nothing more essential and more divine in this world than the Eucharist.*

In prioritizing, not only do things shift when we place God first, but a strong faith life also reveals to us things we can eliminate from our lives completely... perhaps it's a pattern of sin that we could not seem to get out of before, or a toxic friendship, or a tendency to consume media - magazines, television shows, or music

we know just is not filling our eyes, mind, or ears with good things. Journeying with God helps our priorities fall into place because it changes our perspective to see what is most important in life. God will show you how to fill your life with good things. Walk with Him. He will.

Placing God before everything else, however, does not mean we should all be spending our days praying in a chapel and doing nothing else. A life of faith is also a life of balance. When I was in college, I was very a busy broadcast journalism major - God was first on the list but getting great grades in my classes was very important if I wanted to graduate on time and have a successful career in journalism. The balance I found was in dedicating that 30 minutes of daily Mass to God, and then letting God into the rest of my day as I went about my work. I have always loved listening to worship music, and that was a part of my days. I sought out a women's group that met weekly to be in community with one another every Tuesday. We met to share about faith and joined together in prayer but some nights we chose to spend having fun, painting nails, or having dinner parties. My faith was a part of those friendships, because placing God first is not just about a prayer life - faith can be incorporated into every aspect of our daily lives.

What does your list of priorities look like? Does it look like Martha's list, and the list of every home in Bethlehem on the evening of the birth of Christ? Or does it look like Mary's? We all begin to become like the friends we spend time with. Why not make it our number one priority to spend time with God, and in doing so, become more and more like Him with every prayer? He loves you deeply, and wants to be placed first in your life, but will never force you to do so. *It is a gift you must give yourself.*

Make time for the Lord and you will find your life filled with His goodness that knows no end. After all, He has created all the time in the world for you.

PRAYER

Lord, my life tends to get so busy and full. In the midst of the busyness of life, help me to see the importance of putting you first in my life - then give me the courage to take the necessary steps to place you there on my priorities list. When I stray from placing you first, please beckon me back to relationship with you. I ask that you place within me deep desires to pray, to receive the Sacraments frequently, to cultivate faith-filled friendships, and to spend time with you. You are the King of my Heart and the Lord of my life. Help me to always choose the better part. Amen.

REFLECTION

- Do you create a false sense of "busyness" in your life that consumes your being and leaves you feeling unfulfilled or sad? Is there a way you can manage your time better so that you are not always so "busy"?

- What in your life is competing with your relationship with God? Is it your time spent on social media? Is it too much watching TV, or time spent with friends? Can you decide today to reduce or eliminate some things in order to put God first?

GIFTED

TABITHA

Now in Joppa there was a disciple whose name was Tabitha, which in Greek is Dorcas. She was devoted to good works and acts of charity. At that time she became ill and died. When they had washed her, they laid her in a room upstairs. Since Lydda was near Joppa, the disciples, who heard that Peter was there, sent two men to him with the request, "Please come to us without delay." So Peter got up and went with them; and when he arrived, they took him to the room upstairs. All the widows stood beside him, weeping and showing tunics and other clothing that Dorcas had made while she was with them. Peter put all of them outside, and then he knelt down and prayed. He turned to the body and said, "Tabitha, get up." Then she opened her eyes, and seeing Peter, she sat up. He gave her his hand and helped her up. Then calling the saints and widows, he showed her to be alive. This became known throughout Joppa, and many believed in the Lord.

--Acts 9: 36-42

Tabitha had a gift.

Her gift was sewing, which is certainly not a gift that will put anyone on a pedestal or at the center of attention. Our culture does not grant honors or attention for gifts like sewing… but Tabitha shows us that she was a faithful, sewing daughter of God, and her gift makes a beautiful difference.

Our culture commonly views the "gifts" a person possesses to be something wonderfully grand. Someone who is "gifted" is thought to have some sort of exceptional ability or talent in some area that is superior to the talents or lack of talents of others. We praise the giftedness of athletes, musicians, singers, filmmakers, actors, and actresses. Our culture celebrates gifts that put people in the spotlight which tells us that if our "gift" doesn't make us money, it is worthless. If our "gifts" don't get us recognition, they are nothing to pay attention to. God's definition of what a gift is stands in a beautiful opposition our culture's. Each person God creates is "gifted." Every person is born with gifts God places within them to carry out His purpose in their life and in the world.

In St. Paul's letter to the Romans, he highlights the beauty of the different gifts each of us are given:

"For as in one body we have many members, and not all the members have the same function, so we, who are many, are one body in Christ, and individually

we are members of one another. We have gifts that differ according to the grace given to us: prophecy, in proportion to faith; ministry, in ministering; the teacher, in teaching; the exhorter, in exhortation; the giver, in generosity; the leader, in diligence; the compassionate, in cheerfulness" (Romans 12: 4-8).

Consider the boy with the loaves and fishes in the Gospel of John (John 6:9). He is only mentioned in John's Gospel, and when everyone is looking around for something to feed the multitudes of hungry people, Andrew brings to Jesus' attention the loaves and fish that belong to the young boy. I imagine this sweet boy thought, *how would my small lunch ever put a dent in the need of all these people?* But this little boy gives the gift of his small lunch to Jesus, who takes this small gift and multiplies it in the stunning miracle of the loaves and fishes.

This boy's gift was not an ability to sing or dance or make beautiful art. It was not something that would bring him fame or fortune. It was a few loaves of bread and a couple of fish.

The boy had food. Tabitha had fabric. She is regarded as a disciple, which speaks greatly to how faithful she was to God and well-regarded she was as an evangelist in her community. The women who stand at Tabitha's bedside upon her death sorrowfully show Paul the garments she has made them - they show Paul to tell him...*this is the way she loved us.*

We each have certain gifts that God has bestowed specifically upon each one of us. It is likely that these gifts may take on an unexpected form, and upon first reflection it can be difficult to think of what our gifts may be. So how do we figure out what our gifts are? When I reflected on this question long ago in my own life, it brought me to ask myself another question..."How can I make people in this world feel loved?"

It is often in that answer where our gifts lie.

One Friday night, my husband Daniël and I went to a little walk up restaurant and ordered some good Southern food. There was a woman working there who was one of the most positive, upbeat people I have ever seen working at a restaurant. I noticed her from far away, laughing and greeting other guests. I could immediately tell by her spirit, even standing far away, that she loved what she did. She loved making people's experience at this restaurant unforgettable. When we sat down she spoke enthusiastically with us, with such warm hospitality and a totally infectious positivity. This night was over a year ago, and I still remember the impact her upbeat spirit had on our night. That was her gift. Her positive energy and enthusiasm toward what she was doing were meaningful in that one small experience we had in her presence; she knew how to love people for the short time they were in her restaurant.

I want you to believe me when I tell you… you may not be the star of the musical or the cheerleading team. You may not lead some prominent club on campus, and you may lose every single school election you run in (I did!)… *but you have spectacular gifts within your soul.*

Your gift may be sewing. Perhaps it is cooking. Consider the gifts of encouragement, teaching, giving, graphic design, planning and organization, thoughtfulness, music, writing, or gardening. There are thousands of gifts, and God's plan at work needs every one of us to recognize how we can best show love to people in desperate need of it. He needs us to be his hands and feet here on this earth, and one way we do that is by living and breathing our gifts, no matter how small or insignificant they may seem to us.

When we put them in the hands of our all-powerful God, He uses them to work miracles.

PRAYER

God, I know you have placed great gifts within me to share with the world. Thank you for the gifts you have given me. Help me to come to know what those gifts are and how I can best use them to be your hands and feet here on earth. Help me to recognize how I can love people best, and how I can share your love in a world that desperately needs it. Amen.

REFLECTION

- Do you know what your gifts are? If so, what are they, and are you currently using them to bring glory to God?

- If you don't know what your gifts are...ask yourself the question - how can I make people in this world feel loved? Consider the answer and how you can put the answer into motion in your life.

I CHOOSE
THE SKY

THE CRIPPLED WOMAN

Now [Jesus] was teaching in a synagogue on the sabbath. And just then there appeared a woman with a spirit that had crippled her for eighteen years. She was bent over and was quite unable to stand up straight. When Jesus saw her, he called her over and said, "Woman, you are set free from your ailment." When He laid His hands on her, immediately she stood up straight and began praising God. But the leader of the synagogue, indignant because Jesus had cured on the sabbath, kept saying to the crowd, "There are six days on which work ought to be done; come on those days and be cured, and not on the sabbath day." The Lord said to Him in reply, "Hypocrites! Does not each one of you on the sabbath untie his ox or his ass from the manger and lead it out for watering? This daughter of Abraham, whom Satan has bound for eighteen years now, ought she not to have been set free on the sabbath day from this bondage?" When he said this, all his adversaries were humiliated; and the whole crowd rejoiced at all the splendid deeds done by him.

--Luke 13:10-17

Cement, dirt, asphalt, grass, carpet, linoleum. Have you ever thought about the things that you walk on? The brown dust that is dirt, the worn out tiles in your kitchen, the awful forest green carpet in your grandmother's house, or the cracks in the gray sidewalk? There is not much that is wondrous, exciting, or thought-provoking about the ground on which we walk.

This woman spent eighteen years looking at the uninspiring ground because of the spirit that crippled her. She could not look up to see a tree, or a bird, or a beautiful sunset, or the face of the person in front of her. It is likely that she could not even look up to see Jesus as she stood in His presence. Eighteen years of physical suffering is far beyond what many people will experience in a lifetime. Unlike this woman, I am not physically crippled. I can stand up perfectly straight and walk on my two feet, yet this account of her ailment still speaks greatly to me when I look at the posture of my heart.

I have an uncle who, like this crippled woman, has struggled greatly with physical illness throughout his life. He was diagnosed with juvenile diabetes at a young age, has major problems with his kidneys, and recently had a heart attack that nearly took his life. His life has been difficult and challenging, but when you ask him how he is doing, he always responds with the same answer,

"I'm great. Never had a bad day in my life." To anyone who inquires about this response, he will tell them how he has nothing to complain about - he has a great wife who loves him, great children, and God, who keeps providing for him. It would be easy for my uncle to give into hopelessness and despair with the monumental struggles he faces every day. But he refuses to see anything except the positive.

Our perspective and our outlook have an incredible impact on our day-to-day lives. Our perspective dictates how our days seem to go, how we treat others, how we treat ourselves, and how we see the world. We have the power to choose whether we approach life with positivity or negativity. We make the decision to be cheerful, loving, and kind, even when life is challenging... or to give into envy, self-loathing, or despair when we just wish things were different, or better, or easier. We get to decide which outlook we have: Are you looking at the ground, or are you looking up at the sky?

That is the thing about perspective in life - each of us gets to choose. There is power in the outlook we select because we have the power to see the beauty of life in front of us or to cast our gaze downward to the lifeless ground.

The road we choose has everything to do with the posture of our hearts. We cripple our hearts by letting negativity, gossip, and criticism invade our thoughts and actions. We turn our faces downward when we speak uncharitably about another woman, because speaking unkind words keeps us from seeing the beauty in her. We look at the ground when we complain because we do not feel we have enough friends, or things, or followers, or popularity, because our complaining keeps us from seeing all that we are blessed with. We fix our gaze to the ground when we begin the day by tearing ourselves down in the mirror rather than speaking words of life and truth to our own hearts and minds. There are too many times when we choose these things and allow negativity to rule our hearts and steal our joy.

When this woman stood in the presence of the Lord, she could not look up to see him because her posture kept her from doing so. *When we choose pessimism, we place blocks in our hearts to seeing the goodness of God or even recognizing His presence before us.* There is a sadness that comes with living a life completely unaware of beauty, of blessing, of the gift of life. The life of a Christian is not meant to a sad life...it is a life that is meant to be filled with joy, peace, and fulfillment, both on wonderful days and days of suffering. Choosing to fix our eyes on Christ cultivates a cheerful, positive, and generous heart. A life spent in awe of God's goodness, of speaking uplifting words, of sacrificing with joy for others - this is the life and perspective which allows us to look up at Christ before us in our lives.

If given the choice between the ground and the sky, I choose the sky.

PRAYER

Lord, I ask that you cultivate in my heart a perspective of positivity, of gratitude, and of grace. Help me to see the goodness in others and in myself. When my self-image gets me down, when I feel mean-spirited, when I cannot find anything positive to say about others or myself, help me to fix my eyes upon you. Help me to be quick to give thanks rather than to complain, to uplift rather than tear down, and to trust in your goodness on days of joy and days of struggle. Give me a posture of heart that makes way for seeing your blessings, your goodness, and your grace. Amen.

REFLECTION

- Do you consider yourself a woman who dwells in negativity or a woman who dwells on blessings? Are you quick to complain or quick to give thanks? Why?

- Is there an area in your life where you feel you need a change in the posture of your heart? Is it in the way you view yourself? Your tendency to give into hopelessness when things do not go your way? Your jealousy of others? What is the first step to making this change in your life?

RUNNING TO MERCY

THE SINFUL WOMAN

One of the Pharisees asked Jesus to eat with him, and he went into the Pharisee's house and took his place at the table. And a woman in the city, who was a sinner, having learned that he was eating in the Pharisee's house, brought an alabaster jar of ointment. She stood behind him at his feet, weeping, and began to bathe his feet with her tears and to dry them with her hair. Then she continued kissing his feet and anointing them with the ointment.

Now when the Pharisee who had invited him saw it, he said to himself, "If this man were a prophet, he would have known who and what kind of woman this is who is touching him - that she is a sinner." Jesus spoke up and said to him, "Simon, I have something to say to you." "Teacher," he replied, "speak."

"A creditor had two debtors; one owed five hundred denarii, and the other fifty. When they could not pay, he cancelled the debts for both of them. Now which of them will love him more?" Simon answered, "I suppose the one for whom he cancelled the greater debt." And Jesus said to him, "You have judged rightly."

Then turning towards the woman, he said to Simon, "Do you see this woman? I entered your house; you gave me no water for my feet, but she has bathed my feet with her tears and dried them with her hair. You gave me no kiss, but from the time I came in she has not stopped kissing my feet. You did not anoint my head with oil, but she anointed my feet with ointment. Therefore, I tell you, her sins, which were many, have been forgiven; hence she has shown great love. But the one to whom little is forgiven, loves little." Then he said to her, "Your sins are forgiven." But those who were at the table with him began to say among themselves, "Who is this who even forgives sins?"

And he said to the woman, "Your faith has saved you; go in peace."

--Luke 7: 36-50

I want to be like her.

When I read the account of the sinful woman, I know there is much that she and I have in common.

The main commonality we have? Sin. Sin comes in a multitude of forms, with each sin I commit a conscious turning away from God, turning my back on His love, turning my back on the way I know is good. Sin is sin - and this woman and I, we both know it well.

The second commonality she and I share? The choice of what we do in our sin. It is a choice each of us receives... to run toward God or to run away from God.

In the midst of all her grief and shame, in all her embarrassment and sin - she hears that Jesus is in her town. Upon hearing this news, she is faced with two choices... the first is to stay at home. Imagine the dialogue in her head, *"Why would Jesus want to see me? I have messed up too greatly for Him to look on me with love."* Her second choice is to go out and meet Christ where He is, knowing deeply that in her sin, Christ is all she needs. This woman knows well where her need lies and she chooses the latter. She does not hide in her sin, nor does she recoil from Jesus in her shame...instead, *she stops at nothing to get to Him.* She finds the house where Jesus is visiting, goes inside, and showers Him with an enormous outpouring of love born out of deep emotion and genuine sorrow. She fervently seeks Jesus to lavish Him with all the love in her heart.

Oh, how this woman shows us how to seek Christ's mercy with reckless abandon.

She shows us how passionately we are to seek God in the throes of sin and brokenness, and I want to live like her - in this moment - when I experience sorrow and shame. I want my response to be to run to encounter God right where I know He is.

Jesus does not walk this Earth in a physical body today. He does not stop by to have dinner with our neighbors or teach in the streets. But I know where Jesus is in my town. Jesus is present in the Eucharist in a church less than two miles from my house. I can get there in a quick bike ride or drive. I know what time Mass is, I know that the adoration chapel is open 24 hours a day, and I know that the Sacrament of Reconciliation is available on Thursday evenings and twice on Saturdays.

I know where Jesus is, I know where I can rest in His presence and His mercy, but there are too many times when I run the other way. In my human frailty and pride, I rationalize my sin as not being bad enough to enter the confessional. Sometimes I decide that I am too busy, and other times I just cannot look at His body on the crucifix at the front of the Church because I feel I do not deserve mercy for the mess I am making.

But then God beckons me back; He gently tugs on my heart in those moments when I have run and asks me to stop and reflect... how many times have I regretted

running to God in my need? None. How many times have I wished I had not gone to confession? Zero. When have I ever felt that visiting Christ in the adoration chapel was a waste? Never. But in those times when I feel I have let God down and turned away - I am ashamed, I am embarrassed, and I feel like I am a failure.

She may have felt this word - failure - as sin consumed her life over and over again, a cycle she could not seem to free herself from. She may have felt the same words ringing loud in her heart as we do:

Sinner.

Failure.

Shameful.

Unworthy.

Maybe she called herself those names out loud. I have.

In times of deep desperation I have spoken ugly words to myself aloud as I have cried into the mirror, into my pillow, into my hands - words I would never dare speak to another. Words that steal and destroy. Words that are lies from the mouth of the enemy.

She falls at the feet of Christ and showers Him with love, and does He utter any such word...unworthy, unlovable, unforgivable?

No. He calls her woman. He sees her.

"Do you see this woman?" Not failure. Not sinner. Not stupid. Not a mess.

When you wake up in the morning, Jesus sees you. When you go about your day, He sees you. When you walk into the Church - He sees you. When you sit before the priest in the confessional nervous, embarrassed, or filled with shame - He sees *you*.

When you open the door of that small confessional and enter into the Sacrament of Reconciliation, when you sit in that chair across from a priest *in persona Christi*, Jesus Christ looks at you and only sees "woman." He only sees "daughter." He only sees "forgivable." *He only wishes to shower you with love and bestow upon you the power of His mercy.*

Jesus looks upon the sinful woman just as He looks at us and says, "Your sins have been forgiven." Every last one of them.

With the knowledge of this truth, may we live our lives running one way...

Toward love. Toward mercy. Toward Jesus Christ.

His merciful heart is open to each and every one of us.

PRAYER

Lord, I know where I can find you, but sometimes my sin keeps me from running to find you there. When I feel lost, broken, confused, guilty, or shameful, help me to always run to you, the giver of mercy and love. May running to you be my default response in the midst of guilt and shame. Rid my heart of the lies I speak into my own heart and allow me to hear the words of truth you speak into it. When I feel like a failure, let me hear you call me forgiven. When I feel unlovable, open my heart to feel your outpouring of love into my life. Amen.

REFLECTION

- Have there been times in your life where you ran from God in your shame? Where did it leave you?

- Is there an area in your heart that you don't currently want to bring to God? Is there an area in your life right now that is causing you to hide from God? What is it and where can you begin in offering it to Him?

OPEN HEARTS
AND
OPEN HOMES

LYDIA

We sat and spoke with the women who had gathered there. One of them, a woman named Lydia, a dealer in purple cloth, from the city of Thyatira, a worshiper of God, listened, and the Lord opened her heart to pay attention to what Paul was saying. After she and her household had been baptized, she offered us an invitation, "If you consider me a believer in the Lord, come and stay at my home," and she prevailed on us.

--Acts 16:13-15

Baptism is an incredible new beginning. There are a number of life-altering components encompassed in the first Sacrament of Initiation. First, Baptism cleanses a person of their original sin; when a person is washed with the holy water, the stain of sin every human is born with is completely washed away. Baptism also marks a person permanently as a son or daughter of God; they become an eternal member of the Body of Christ. Within a person's baptism, they also receive the call to be a disciple in the world and to spread the truth of Christ's life, death, and Resurrection. Baptism changes the course of a person's life, so we can imagine Lydia's thrill at being baptized because of her deep and heartfelt devotion to the Lord. If you have never attended, go to an Easter Vigil at least once in your life and watch adults thrilled to step into the holy water font and have this blessed water poured over their heads. Watching a baby get baptized is a wonderful thing, as the baby's parents choose for the baby to be a part of our faith and to receive the indelible mark of Christ on their soul. Watching adults be baptized into our Catholic faith takes on a new layer of magnificence - watching people who have fallen so in love with Christ, who recognize Catholicism as truth and desire to be a part of our great Church... it is a spectacular thing to witness their joy at their deeply life-altering decision to receive this sacrament.

Where Lydia inspires me in this account is her response to her Baptism. After she is baptized, she desires to serve God in any way possible. She does not stop to think for long. She does not spend time mulling over what her gifts are or how she can serve; she immediately offers a simple invitation to Paul and Timothy to stay in her home, an offer of wholehearted hospitality and giving.

Her immediate enthusiasm to serve causes me to ask myself, is faith a stagnant fact in my life or do I allow my deep love for Christ to motivate me to serve others?

We live in a culture that is almost entirely focused on self before service. For so many, giving to others takes a back seat after dealing with our own problems, troubles, needs, wants, and more...which is why it leaves me in awe to witness the kind of people who serve with an openness that does not measure.

I know a man who has allowed his love for Christ to motivate him to a hospitality of incredibly sacrificial love. His name is Stephen, and he is one of the most saintly individuals I know. While sitting with Stephen one day, he began to tell me about how early on in his marriage, he and his wife were given the opportunity to take in a very troubled young woman and do what they could to help her. They welcomed the opportunity to serve and help this young woman as newlyweds. What Stephen and his wife did not know was that this young woman would be the first of dozens of foster children they would welcome into their home over

many years. They opened their hearts and home to put many young people in great need before themselves - answering God's call to hospitality in an immeasurable way. The impact that their hospitality had on these many foster children's lives is unfathomable - the ripples that their welcoming home spread through these children goes beyond calculation. Stephen has spent many years of his life serving the poor in Haiti and in Africa, serves thousands of teens at Catholic summer camps, and is a light to all who meet him because of his devout love and dedication to the Lord. Because of his faith, Stephen is eager to serve. Because of his faith, Stephen cannot help but open his heart to everyone he meets.

So as I reflect on the lives of those like Lydia and Stephen, I ask myself: Am I motivated by my faith to serve others? To open my heart? To open my home? To put others before myself without even thinking twice?

These individuals both humbly share their gift of hospitality. However, there is a common misconception that hospitality requires a dining room so that people can join you for dinner or a home for people to stay in. Hospitality is not only a physical gift, but it is a gift that can and should be practiced by our hearts. Has there ever been a woman in your life who makes everyone around her feel welcome in every situation? In a new place, in a group of friends, at church? She is always kind, inclusive, and friendly, and everyone in her community probably knows her as that loving woman characterized by the beautiful qualities of friendliness and warmth. The women who leave this memorable mark on others are open-hearted, and hospitality at its core has everything to do with open heartedness and inclusivity. These women who live out hospitality with their open hearts are the ones who begin conversations with new people, who show an interest in a new person joining their youth group, sports team, or class, and who are aware of including everyone around them.

As daughters of God, we are forever called to be that unmistakable woman who makes other people feel included and welcome in our presence.

We are called as Christians to this open heartedness because it is what Jesus practiced...an openness to all - sinners and saints alike. This is exactly what Lydia did. She had the means to practice both physical hospitality and the hospitality of her heart, and she welcomed Paul and Timothy in both ways without a moment of hesitation.

How can we live hospitality as young women? It begins in the simplest of ways. How about reaching out to the girl at school who no one seems to talk to? An invitation to eat with your friends or hang out on a Friday night would probably mean more to her than she could ever express. What about sending a card to thank a teacher who has helped you tremendously?

Perhaps you could spend one day a week or month volunteering at an organization that makes a difference in the lives of people in need. Another way to show hospitality is to always be willing to lend a hand and offer to help in every situation, rather than sitting back and allowing others to complete a task. Whether that is for one of your parents, a teacher, a friend - a helping hand and willingness to sacrifice is always reflective of an open and generous heart.

Recently, while standing in line at a grocery store, I noticed a girl who was probably eight years old checking out with her mom. As the groceries were scanned, without being asked, this tiny girl began opening up brown paper bags and loading up the groceries for her mom. This sweet girl was showing her hospitable heart at a young age. Hospitality does not often require much of us, but it is a powerful character trait that, if practiced often enough, will become a part of who we are as women and affect our lives in a very positive way.

The call to hospitality and charity is a challenging one, because as Christ's disciples we are called to have open hearts to more than just our friends or those who are lonely or in need. As disciples, we are called to extend our open-heartedness to those we find most difficult to love. It is challenging to make someone feel welcome in our presence who we do not get along with or who has hurt us, or to show any sign of warmth to them. Yet, that is the essence of life in

Christ - loving those who, in our own humanity, we could never love by ourselves.

It is and will always be the power of Christ alive within us that makes loving and reaching out to our enemies possible.

So, that person who seems to continually rub you the wrong way? Break down walls with your friendliness and openness - begin a conversation with them. That sibling of yours who you just cannot get along with? Pray that God would help you love them the way He does. Find the same good in them that God sees in you. When we humbly ask the Lord to help us love those we find it most difficult to love, it is in those moments that we become more holy, more loving, and more like Christ.

We can each practice hospitality in many moments of our everyday lives. Incredible things happen when we open our hearts to love and serve others. Walk daily with the Lord, and with all the graces given to you in baptism, allow it to help you walk in charity. We can each be that woman people remember for her loving and open heart, and more importantly, we can all be the women who spread Christ's warmth and joy to every person we meet.

PRAYER

God, I ask that you give me a heart of hospitality. Help me to continually be a woman who is warm, loving, and inviting - all the things that you were in your time here on earth. Give me a heart of inclusion - give me eyes to see the people in my life who need to be invited into places or groups where I already belong. May people always leave my presence feeling welcomed, may they always leave my presence feeling your love. When I find it hard to open my heart and home, give me Lydia's heart and help me to open it as a witness to your generosity and love. Amen.

REFLECTION

- Think about the most hospitable woman you know in your life. What is it about her hospitality that makes you see her as such? Where can you be inspired in your own life by the way she lives hers?

- Do you live a life of complacent faith, or do you take the call to hospitality into serious practice in your life? How well are you practicing hospitality of your heart and home?

SPEAK UP

THE DAUGHTERS OF
ZELOPHEHAD

Then the daughters of Zelophehad came forward...the names of his daughters were: Mahlah, Noah, Hoglah, Milcah, and Tirzah. They stood before Moses, Eleazar the priest, the leaders, and all the congregation, at the entrance of the tent of meeting, and they said, "Our father died in the wilderness, he was not among the company of those who gathered themselves together against the Lord in the company of Korah, but died for his own sin; and he had no sons. Why should the name of our father be taken away from his clan because he had no son? Give to us a possession among our father's brothers."

Moses brought their case before the Lord. And the Lord spoke to Moses, saying: The daughters of Zelophehad are right in what they are saying; you shall indeed let them possess an inheritance among their father's brothers and pass the inheritance of their father on to them. You shall also say to the Israelites, "If a man died, and has no son, then you shall pass his inheritance on to his daughter. If he has no daughter, then you shall give his inheritance to his brothers. If he has no brothers, then you shall give his inheritance to his father's brothers. And if his father has no brothers, then you shall give his inheritance to the nearest kinsman of his clan, and he shall possess it. It shall be for the Israelites a statute and ordinance," as the Lord commanded Moses.

--Numbers 27: 1-11

When I was a senior in high school, I wanted to go to my school's winter formal. I attended an all-girls Catholic high school, and the requirement for going to the dance was that you needed to have a date; a guy from another school must agree to go with you. Between school, sports, musicals, etc., my friends and I did not spend a lot of time with guys, so we thought the requirement was unfair. Instead of searching for guys to bring, we scheduled an appointment with the school principal to express our thoughts. We had a meeting with her, and another two meetings with a few more administrators and expressed our belief that if we go to an all-girls school, we should be able to attend the dance solo. After a few weeks of back and forth, the administration agreed and a new rule was passed. From our senior year on, girls were able to attend the dance by themselves if they so desired. Five friends and I went to formal together - we bought $25 dresses from Forever 21 and rode in our friend's beat up forest green Chrysler van to the dance - and we had the time of our lives.

A few years later, I worked as campus minister at this high school. When winter formal rolled around, I took great delight in asking my students whether they were going with a date or going solo. They were able to choose between the two options because my friends and I decided to use our voices to make a small change in our little community.

The daughters of Zelophehad - Mahlah, Noah, Hoglah, Milcah, and Tirzah - decided to do the same thing. They chose to step up and use their voices to make a change. When their father died, because they were women and not men, they were not qualified to receive his inheritance. They saw this injustice, and in great bravery stood before Moses and the other leaders in the community to speak up for what they believe is right.

Moses and the leaders bring their point to the Lord, and a change is made. They are able, as women, to receive their father's inheritance - it becomes law that if a man only has a daughter upon his death, she receives what is rightfully hers as the child of the deceased. Had they not spoken up, there is no telling if or when the law ever would have been made different.

The previous policy on winter formal dates at my high school was not a huge injustice - but it was an issue we recognized we could do something about. You and I live in a world ridden with true and extreme injustice. We live in a world that kills the unborn, the sick, and the dying. We live in a time where people still turn a blind eye to the starving, when countless women are regularly sold into trafficking, when refugees are fleeing unthinkable war. Injustice is a part of our every day.

With the storms of injustice raging around us, we can too easily become disheartened and discouraged. *How can I, as one person, make any difference? How can we use our voices in the midst of the deafening noise of the injustice which surrounds us?*

I find hope alive and well in our world in witnessing our peers using their voices in extremely important ways. There are countless young people beginning influential movements, holding peaceful rallies, donating their time, money, or talents to charities and organizations that create critical changes for the ignored and oppressed in our world. They are living radical lives as champions and advocates for the broken, bruised, and forgotten.

Every January, I witness people using their voices against injustice for the most vulnerable of us all. The March for Life is a powerful event that happens every year on the anniversary of the Roe v. Wade decision to legalize abortion in the United States. This peaceful walk intended to bring change to legislation regarding abortion drew nearly one million people in 2015. It is estimated that about half of the marchers are under the age of thirty. Young people are using their voices, their presence, their conviction to create change in our world...they are exhibiting their passion to help citizens and politicians across America, one by one, realize the dignity of every human life.

They are standing up for the forgotten who cannot stand up for themselves.

I also follow a girl named Hannah and her life adventures online. Hannah has shown me a completely unique way to use her voice to stand up for an injustice she feels very passionately about. A few years ago, Hannah became aware of the massive problem that millions of people in the world have of obtaining clean water. Children and women in many poor countries must walk miles to fill up a big yellow plastic gasoline can with clean water every day for their home; something in America we cannot fathom as we turn on a hot shower or faucet with the twist of a knob. When she learned about this injustice, Hannah felt an immediate desire in her heart to help people in these countries obtain easier access to clean water. One day she decided to carry one of these cans filled with water herself, and found it extremely difficult. She wanted to truly experience the plight of people who must fill this can up and walk with it every day, so she began to carry the can everywhere she went. She carried this "jerry can" to school, to the gym, out with friends - and this was her creative way to use her voice to speak up against a crisis she wanted to do something about. People would stop to ask her why she was carrying this huge yellow gasoline can, and it gave her an opportunity to bring others to awareness of the clean water crisis. Hannah has not stopped using her voice on this issue ever since. She used this can to start a club of 70 students at her university dedicated to fundraising for countries to gain better access to clean water and building wells. She has raised over 10,000 dollars to help communities and their projects to build wells. She also gave an inspiring talk at her university about her journey from day one. Hannah used a yellow can to make a change. She uses her voice daily to speak up for the forgotten people in the world she feels strongly about. Her voice is making waves and helping thousands of people gain access to a healthy life with clean water.

Watch Jesus closely in the Gospels, and let us not forget who He lifted up. He stood in defense of those in greatest need of love - prostitutes, adulterers, tax collectors, lepers... *our King spoke up for them all.* We can follow the example Jesus illustrated in His life, or we can be quiet if we so choose. We can live comfortable lives of silence and cold shoulders toward those who need someone to speak up for them; it is surely easier not to do anything about the injustice we see. However, the call to Christian love and outreach is not easy. It is a call to love that stretches us beyond the limits we think we have - and it is a call directly from the God who showed us how to love the lost and least. We, as Catholic Christians, must follow the lead of our God alive here on earth who spoke up and defended the most broken of all.

A ripple effect begins with one person. Your voice and your actions possess great power. Your commitment to making a change in this world or in the life of one person can exceed far beyond what you ever dreamed possible.

So what will you use your one life to do - stay silent or speak up?

PRAYER

Lord, in this world I am surrounded by tough issues, heartbreaking situations, and terrible injustice. Sometimes I do not know where to begin in fighting for change or for what I believe in, but I know you brought me into existence to make positive changes in the world. Help me to realize what I am most passionate about, where I can best give my time and efforts to help those in need, and where to begin. Give me your heart for the lost, the poor, and the forgotten. I want my one life to make a difference, and I know I can only do that by your courage and strength within me. Give me the bravery to speak up in whatever form that may take. Amen.

REFLECTION

- Is there an injustice you see - large or small scale - that makes you think, "I want to do something about this"? What is that injustice?

- Are you sitting back and waiting for someone else to do something? Or are you ready to speak up and do something about this injustice yourself? Write down some ways you make be able to take a first small step in committing to doing something about this issue.

A GLIMMER
OF HOPE

THE HEMORRHAGING
WOMAN

Now there was a woman who had been suffering from hemorrhages for twelve years. She had endured much under many physicians, and had spent all that she had; and she was no better, but rather grew worse. She had heard about Jesus, and came up behind him in the crowd and touched his cloak, for she said, "If I but touch his clothes, I will be made well." Immediately her hemorrhage stopped; and she felt in her body that she was healed of her disease. Immediately aware that power had gone forth from him, Jesus turned about in the crowd and said, "Who touched my clothes?" And his disciples said to him, "You see the crowd pressing in on you; how can you say, 'Who touched me?'" He looked all round to see who had done it. But the woman, knowing what had happened to her, came in fear and trembling, fell down before him, and told him the whole truth. He said to her, "Daughter, your faith has made you well; go in peace, and be healed of your disease."

--Mark 5: 25-34

We do not know her name, her age, or her history. We only know that she was a woman in pain and Jesus stopped for her.

This woman suffered for twelve years with a bleeding cancer. Twelve years is an incredibly long time to be suffering such extreme pain. She had spent all her money trying to get help, went to as many doctors as she could, and no one could help her. No one could find a cure. No one could give her any hope for recovering.

But in her heart she never gave up hope of being healed. How do we know this?

She left her home to go see Jesus when word was out he was in town. Her story is very similar to that of the sinful woman who leaves her home to find Jesus. If this woman had given up faith in God's power, she would have stayed home. She would not have considered stepping outside because all options for healing, for a better life, had been exhausted... *What can He do for me? It is hopeless, I have tried everything. I will never be healed.*

But a glimmer of hope remains in her heart and this small flicker of light propels her to leave her home. This glimmer gives her the faith to approach Jesus Christ with unwavering confidence in His ability to heal her and transform her life. She sees Jesus passing by in the dense crowd and as He walks by, she grabs

His garment. She knows that the Messiah has both perfect timing and perfect power, and that this perfect power transforms and heals. And in that moment, her moment of unstoppable faith, the power of God heals her instantly. Her hope and her faith in God save her life.

When I am desperate for healing, love, peace, mercy... do I approach my God with this same unwavering confidence and faith?

We all experience pain in life. For some of us it is physical, for some it is emotional, spiritual, or mental. We all have pain and we each get to choose how we respond to pain. We can respond to our pain by giving up hope, giving into despair, and even losing faith that God exists. Or we can allow our pain to move us, to propel us to reach out to our King.

Reaching out to God when we are hurting can seem uncomfortable and inconvenient. Sometimes reaching out to God means doing more in our prayer life... sometimes it looks like asking others for help in our time of need.

A few years ago, I experienced incredible sorrow as I watched my mentor, Mrs. Nick, die from cancer. Her second battle with cancer lasted thirteen painful months. During this time, I was undoubtedly confused and upset with God. Mrs. Nick was only in her early sixties and was doing such incredible good for young

women; she had not even become a grandmother yet, a gift she greatly longed for. In my pain, I had a really difficult time approaching and reaching out to God; not only was I busy carrying on the campus ministry program at the school, I did not understand why she, who had dedicated her life to the Lord, had to suffer so severely at the end of her life. I was busy and sorrowful. I was bewildered and grieving. I wanted to wake up, go to work, and then come home and go to bed - but on many days I forced myself to go to church and to pray. When I went to Eucharistic adoration, I did not even have words to utter to the Lord, all I could do was weep. But I knew the answer to my pain was reaching out to God. So, no matter how much I did not want to talk with the God who was taking my friend away, I prayed. I prayed for Mrs. Nick's peace, comfort, and strength, and for my trust in God to prevail even in the storm. These times of prayer were uncomfortable because the storms of life were raging and I was not happy with God's will - but prayer is never about being comfortable - it is about reaching out to God who is good even in the midst of tremendous suffering.

God's ways are not our ways (Isaiah 55:8). We may not understand such pain here on earth, but Jesus stops for this woman and for you in your pain, whatever form that takes. Jesus wants to stop for you. *He will stop for you.* He is ever-present and yearns for you to reach out to Him and take hold of His garments.

The hemorrhaging woman reached out to grab Jesus' clothes and as she grasped them, we can almost hear her saying, "Jesus...I need you. Jesus, I believe in your power to transform my life. Be with me now."

Perhaps you find yourself in incredible despair. Reach out to our Savior. He is nearby. Within our faith, we believe that God is omnipresent - present everywhere all at the same time. This is a reality that is tough to wrap our human minds around, but where you are sitting right now, He is with you. He is not looking for formality; He simply asks to be your friend. How do you experience God's presence sitting right where you are? Quiet yourself, and tell God you are listening. Ask Him to help you know of His deep love. Share with Him your thoughts, joys, and fears like you would with a friend. He is present. Go to Him, and speak the same words to Him in confidence that He listens...

Jesus, I need you. I believe in your power to transform my life. Be with me now.

PRAYER

God, there are times in my life when I do not understand your timing. There are times when I suffer and I do not understand why I have to endure such suffering. In times of pain in my life, help me to never lose hope in your timing and power. I trust in your timing, and I trust in your power to heal. I know that you will never leave or forsake me - I ask that you give me the confidence in your power to continually reach out to you in times of joy and in times of great need. Jesus, I need you. I believe in your power to transform my life. Be with me now. Amen.

REFLECTION

- Is there an area in your life where you have given up on believing that Christ can heal? Upon reflecting on the hemorrhaging woman, are you moved to regain hope and confidence in God's timing and healing power?

- What is a prayer that you have been waiting on God to answer? If you have not yet received an answer, is it because God has answered you differently than you hoped for? If you are still waiting, pray your intention again. God is always listening.

STEADFAST
FRIENDSHIP

RUTH

"Then she started to return with her daughters-in-law from the country of Moab, for she had heard in the country of Moab that the Lord had had consideration for his people and given them food. So she set out from the place where she had been living, she and her two daughters-in-law, and they went on their way to go back to the land of Judah. But Naomi said to her two daughters-in-law, "Go back each of you to your mother's house. May the Lord deal kindly with you, as you have dealt with the dead and with me. The Lord grant that you may find security, each of you in the house of your husband." Then she kissed them, and they wept aloud. They said to her, "No, we will return with you to your people." But Naomi said, "Turn back, my daughters, go your way, for I am too old to have a husband. Even if I thought there was hope for me, even if I should have a husband tonight and bear sons, would you then wait until they were grown? Would you then refrain from marrying? No, my daughters, it has been far more bitter for me than for you, because the hand of the Lord has turned against me." Then they wept aloud again. Orpah kissed her mother-in-law, but Ruth clung to her.

So she said, "See, your sister-in-law has gone back to her people and to her gods; return after your sister-in-law." But Ruth said,

"Do not press me to leave you or to turn back from following you! Wherever you go, I will go; where you lodge, I will lodge; Your people shall be my people, and your God my God. Where you die, I will die -- there will I be buried. May the Lord do thus and so to me, and more as well, if even death parts me from you!"

When Naomi saw that she was determined to go with her, she said no more to her.

--Ruth 1: 6-18

In the book of Ruth, this heroic woman exemplifies the love that each woman is called to show her friends. When she loses her husband and sons, Naomi leaves to go back to the land of Judah, and her two daughters-in-law accompany her. Into the journey, Naomi tells Orpah and Ruth to return home instead of making the journey with her. Ruth could have abandoned Naomi, but did not hesitate for a second to give a response of deep loyalty and love.

In a world of surface communication, friendship, and conditional love, this fact remains...true friendship will always be rooted in unwavering loyalty. Jesus lived and died in the perfect illustration of true friendship, and said it to his disciples, "No one has greater love than this, to lay down one's life for one's friends." (John 15:13 NAB)

Hundreds of years before He spoke them, Ruth lived Jesus' words with her life. Ruth was willing to lay down her life to stay with Naomi.

"Where you go I will go; where you lodge, I will lodge; your people shall be my people, and your God my God. Where you die, I will die - there I will be buried. May the Lord do thus and so to me, and more as well, if even death parts me from you!" (Ruth 1:16)

Loyalty resounds in Ruth's declaration.

People who do not know the origin of this Scripture verse, would probably be surprised that this is a declaration from a daughter-in-law to a mother-in-law. It is a promise between two friends - two women who know the depth that the bond of friendship can reach.

When we witness Ruth and Naomi's journey, we do not know the disagreements they may have had or the tension that ever could have occurred between them. As you may well know from your own experiences, good friendships that stand the test of time always see obstacles. But Ruth shows what it means to be true to the bonds of sisterhood when the going gets tough. She stands by Naomi, she fights for her, and she loves her with a deep compassion and a steadfast generosity of heart.

It is unlikely that you will have a friend who goes on a long journey where you will be called to accompany her, but Ruth illustrates what it means to be committed to friends when they go through hard seasons of life... struggles with health, loss of a parent's job, death of a loved one, self-esteem issues, struggles in school, complications with relationships, and more. As women, life can throw us challenging curveballs, and we need friends to share in the joys and to lean on in life's sorrows. This is loyalty. Faithfulness in friendship is the bond that keeps relationships together - it is the glue that helps friends navigate through difficult times, and forging through hard times makes this

bond stronger. Friendships built on genuine loyalty have deep, lasting roots.

When a friend goes through difficult times, loyalty can be expressed in friendship by simply listening - by being truly present. Recently, I was at coffee with my friend, Colleen, and we were discussing the best ways to support a friend in hard times. She said something that struck me and will remain with me forever: "I always want my friends to know they can share their hardships with me. And, if there is one sentence I could say to help them know this, it would be,

'I am comfortable with you sharing your pain with me; talk about it to me.'

This one sentence moved me - what openness it can immediately create between two people, between a woman who needs to be heard and a woman willing to listen. This sentence reflects great commitment to being present to a friend in painful times. Do not undervalue the power of listening.

Another way to show loyalty to a friend is by praying for them and with them. Sometimes it is difficult to pray when we feel lost and tired; we just cannot seem to find the words. A loyal friend carries her friends with her prayers. Offer to pray with a friend who is experiencing struggle; prayer is better than any plate of cupcakes you could ever make her in her time of need, even though most friends will always appreciate baked goods. Other ways to show loyalty are by sharing encouraging words or through small acts of service, like writing a card or taking her to lunch. Thoughtfulness is a powerful gift that goes a long way in times of need or sorrow.

There is a fine line, though, between staying loyal to a friend and remaining in a friendship that is not good for you. It takes a careful heart to recognize the difference in our lives as young women. It is not imperative that every single one of our friends believe exactly what we believe or share in all our interests or activities, but many young women wonder about the point where it is okay or necessary to let a friendship go. When a friendship is really hurting us, hurting our prayer lives, shifting the hands of our moral compass... the first person you must remain loyal to is yourself. It is likely that you have been or will experience a situation where you will consider what to do when a friend strays from her values. We are called to be the sturdy shelter for our friend and to be there for her to guide her and speak truth into her life - until the point when walking with her is causing us to stray from who we are. That is the point where it is necessary to walk away. That is the point where faithfulness to yourself and God trump your loyalty in friendship.

Another situation that is difficult to navigate in light of loyalty is when our friends are struggling and we have the opportunity to get them help. When I was in high school, I had a good friend named Katie. During

our senior year, it became very obvious that Katie was losing weight very rapidly. Other people began to notice and the worry about Katie's health began to escalate. When we would check in on her well-being, she would shrug it off and act like nothing was going on, but I knew in my heart there was something serious happening with her. I considered what loyalty meant during that time and asked myself, *"Is loyalty in this friendship keeping her secret and not saying anything? Or is being a good friend to Katie bringing this to the attention of an adult?"*

Sometimes it is necessary to do hard things to uphold the duty of being a good friend. Sometimes it is imperative that we do things we know our friends will not like, but which put their well-being above everything. I knew that it was my responsibility as a friend to take my concerns to someone we could trust at the school. I knew it was a decision Katie would probably not be very happy with, but I knew that her health was more important than her being upset or angry with me. I got together with another one of our friends and we went to the vice principal. She was a wonderful, trustworthy, caring lady and it was my gut instinct that she was the one we were to take our concerns to. We let her know what we had seen and experienced with Katie's behaviors, eating patterns, and weight. She thanked us for coming to her and told us she would take it from there.

A few weeks passed and Katie stopped talking to us. She ate lunch with different people and didn't associate with us at all anymore. The vice principal had met with her and her parents and began the process of getting Katie to health. Her anger about our decision to bring this to the attention of adults caused her to cut us off as friends. Strangely, it did not make me sad - in this instance, my loyalty to her called me to do something really hard, but incredibly worthwhile. She needed help badly and as her friends, if she was unwilling to get help herself, it was our responsibility to step up and get it for her.

Unfortunately, stories of stepping up to the difficult times of being a friend do not always have happy endings. We never rekindled our friendship with Katie, nor did she ever come back to tell us that we did what was right or thank us for getting her help, which was okay with us because we came to see that the happy ending in situations like this is the knowing that what you did was right, no matter the cost.

Friendship between women is a multi-faceted jewel. It is a very precious thing. Friendships that stand for years have their ups and downs, but when it does get challenging, we look to Ruth. We look to her loyalty and her steadfast love. She shows us what it means to be a friend. She reveals to us the magnificent depths of love and sacrifice that sisterhood can reach.

PRAYER

God, I thank you for Ruth's beautiful example of steadfast loyalty and friendship. I ask that you help me to be a loyal friend. When my friends go through challenging times, give me the courage and patience to stand by them. If ever I worry for a friend's safety, please help me do what is right as a good friend, even when it is difficult. I pray that you bring good, holy, and loving friends into my life who support me and love me for who I am and who you created me to be. Amen.

REFLECTION

- What kind of friend are you? Are you like Ruth - steadfast, loyal, and true to sisterhood even when the going gets rough? Or do you treat friendship like a one-way street, pouring out your problems and needs to friends and closing your heart and ears when they need your friendship in return?

- Do you have a friend who was with you through a really hard time? Consider writing a note or letter to her to thank her for her loyalty in your friendship.

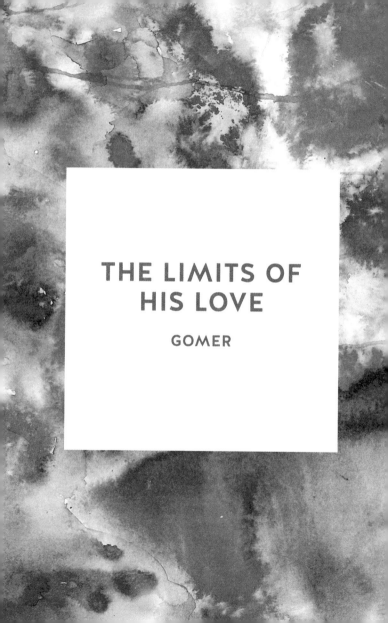

THE LIMITS OF HIS LOVE

GOMER

When the Lord first spoke through Hosea, the Lord said to Hosea, "Go, take for yourself a wife of whoredom and have children of whoredom, for the land commits great whoredom by forsaking the Lord." So he went and took Gomer daughter of Diblaim, and she conceived and bore Him a son.

The Lord said to me again, "Go, love a woman who has a lover and is an adulteress, just as the Lord loves the people of Israel, though they turn to other gods and love raisin cakes." So I bought her for fifteen shekels of silver and a homer of barley and a measure of wine. And I said to her, "You must remain as mine for many days; you shall not play the whore, you shall not have intercourse with a man, nor I with you."

--Hosea 1:2-3; 3:1-3

Hosea stopped at nothing to show Gomer his love.

Christ stops at nothing to show us His love. *His pursuit of our hearts is relentless.*

Relentless, persistent, constant, continual, unceasing, never-ending.

His desire for you to love Him in return will never end.

His love for you has no limits and no measures.

No. Matter. What.

Gomer was living a life of sin and despair as a prostitute when the Lord asked Hosea to take her as his wife. He responded to God's call by marrying Gomer, but what followed was a lot of running. Gomer ran away from Hosea and his love time after time after time. God continually asked Hosea to go and find her and bring her back. It sounds almost ridiculous when you break it down into plain language...Hosea married a prostitute and she kept showing him that she did not want to be with him, but he kept pursuing her and bringing her back to their home anyway. It sounds nearly insane and people most likely thought Hosea was crazy for it.

This story is frequently used to paint an allegory of the masterpiece of God's love for us. It is shown to reflect the resounding truth that even while we were still sinners, Christ died for us (Romans 5:8). He gave us redemption when it was undeserved. He pursues our hearts when we run the other way at full speed. Hosea pursued Gomer when she had wrecked it all. And she ran from this love. She ran and she ran because how is it possible to be loved so much in all her sin?

Maybe you can commiserate. I know I can; I have done the same. I have run from God's love because my human heart just cannot fathom it, this thought of *truly* and *completely* unconditional love. I have experienced many moments of conditional love in life within my friendships and relationships. We will all experience conditional love at some point in our lives - whether that is from our parents, siblings, friends, grandparents. Love with conditions hinders our ability to perceive the truth that God's love is unrestricted. Have you experienced those hurtful moments in relationships when the love runs out, or ends when the going gets tough, or a disagreement hits, or when someone messes up? Our understanding of Christ's love can be distorted in our minds because of these human experiences of conditional love.

The Father's truly and completely limitless love has seen me through moments in my deepest, darkest sin where I have thought, there is no way that God can still love me or still want me. I have done too much, I have willfully disobeyed His commandments in every way - *this "unending" love must have some sort of limit on it and I am sure that I am far past it.*

On a recent retreat, the pastor at my church told a story of a woman who knocked on the door of the parish rectory early in the morning. She was beside herself in tears - she had stopped by the church for the first time in a long time but felt unworthy of even entering through the doors. She felt her sin was too great to be deserving of entry into the house of the Lord. And with all the love and mercy God shows each one of us, our pastor shared how he gently took her right through the doors of our beautiful church and showed her Christ on the cross and spoke His love into her life. He told her she was worthy. He told her that mercy does not run out. He told her of the limitless love of our good God.

And in the darkest times in my life... when I stop running in all my feelings of unworthiness and look back to my Savior, He always whispers the same words to me...

You cannot go past the limits of my love.

You and I, my sister, we cannot pass the limits of His love. It is an absolute and miraculous impossibility. His love does not have limits or boundaries or ends. If you have lied, stolen, or cheated you have not gone past the limits. If you have given into spreading gossip or rumors or being cruel to others, you have not reached the end. If you have spent weeks, months, or years focused entirely on yourself, your looks, and your happiness... if you have spent weekend after weekend drunk with hazy memories and piles of painful regrets... if you have laid in bed next to many men, given up your body time and time again in search of love and acceptance, you have not exited the boundaries of His love. If you have killed his creation inside of you and turned to abortion rather than bringing the life he placed within you into the world, He is still there. He has not forsaken you. He is still loving you. There are no limits. There are none. There will never be any.

And there will never be a time that God stops loving you. There will never be a time when God stops pursuing you. I want you to know this deep down in your bones, sister. *You cannot cause Him to give up on you.*

You and I, we get to live our lives in response to this astonishing, unrelenting love. The arms of the Father are always open. We get to decide whether we keep running away from our home in His heart or if we decide to stay there to accept this love, to accept this mercy, to collapse into His arms of grace when we feel like we have ruined it all, when we are drowning in regret, and when we feel like there is no way Home.

He continually reaches out His hand and offers us a road back. Are you willing to take His hand and come back home?

PRAYER

God, I know that you are always pursuing my heart - even in the midst of my running and brokenness and shame. I ask that you help me be open to your pursuit - soften my heart to be open to the ways you want to reveal your love to me and the ways you reveal your presence in my life. I know that you are and always will be my way Home; help me to reach out to you in times of great struggle and open my ears to hear you whisper your limitless love for me in my heart every day of my life. Amen.

REFLECTION

- Has there ever been a time in your life when you felt you had passed the limits of God's love? How did God reveal his relentless love for you during that time?

- Are you currently in a place where you feel your sin is too great for God to love you? What are those sins and what can Gomer's story teach you about God's love for you even in the midst of sin?

THE BEST THINGS

EVE

Now the serpent was more crafty than any other wild animal that the Lord God had made. He said to the woman, "Did God say, 'You shall not eat from any tree in the garden'?" The woman said to the serpent, "We may eat of the fruit of the trees in the garden; but God said, 'You shall not eat of the fruit of the tree that is in the middle of the garden, nor shall you touch it, or you shall die.'" But the serpent said to the woman, "You will not die; for God knows that when you eat of it your eyes will be opened, and you will be like God, knowing good and evil." So when the woman saw that the tree was good for food, and that it was a delight to the eyes, and that the tree was to be desired to make one wise, she took of its fruit and ate; and she also gave some to her husband, who was with her, and he ate. Then the eyes of both were opened, and they knew that they were naked; and they sewed fig leaves together and made loincloths for themselves.

--Genesis 3: 1-7

As a young person living in a secular culture, have you ever thought to yourself...why does following God and His commandments feel so restrictive? Why does it seem like not following God would allow me so much more freedom? Sometimes in our feeble, frail, and prideful humanity it can get tiring to abide by God's laws.

We start to wonder, and we start to doubt - and that is right where the enemy wiggles in to magnify the whispers just as he did with Eve: *Yes, God is holding out on you. You will be happier if you go your own way instead of God's way. Following God is keeping you from a life of freedom.*

And we know where that led Eve in the Garden of Eden.

Eve begins to believe in her heart and mind that God is keeping something wonderful from her for no apparent reason. The serpent speaks the lie that it brings God joy to withhold the best things from her. She believes it, and she acts on this belief. Upon this action, she brings about the fall of mankind. She brings original sin into existence because she doubts the goodness of God.

Do you ever doubt, like Eve, that God is all-good and all-loving?

We doubt God's goodness in our own lives because the same enemy - the devil - which brought about the fall still prowls the world in an attempt to get each of us to turn away from God (1 Peter 5:8). This enemy will do everything he can to convince you that our God is not kind. He will try to get you to believe that God made His commandments and precepts to make your life miserable and hard. He will attempt to convince you that everyone else who is not following God is having more success, more fun, and more freedom.

Lies.

Not only will the enemy try to get you to believe that we follow an unkind God, the enemy will creep in and tell you that sin is not sin. He will tell you that you are living a less exciting life than everyone else, that you are uncool for being the one girl who is not having sex with her boyfriend, that you are a loser for not going to the parties, that gossip is not wrong, it's fun. He will sneak into many places in your mind and try to get you to believe that not only is God not good - *He is oppressive.*

But the truth that the devil and the world are trying to hide from you is this...*A life following Christ and His commandments is a life that sets us free.*

Eve was given a choice in the garden, and it was not a choice she had to make with unclear instructions - God instructed very clearly, "You shall not eat the fruit of the tree that is in the middle of the garden" (Genesis 2:16-17). She submitted to temptation and humankind became bound by original sin. Following God's commandments frees us from the chains that

enslave us when we are caught up in sin and worldly pleasure. God's ways free us from living lives full of regret, sadness, and control that come from the sins the world convinces us are normal behavior - gossip, vanity, greed, drinking, drugs, sex, pornography, the list goes on.

God's laws liberate us to be who He created us to be.

I want you to believe this because I have struggled with knowing this in my heart through different seasons of life... it brings God joy to give you the best things. In the garden of Eden, Satan's lies were too resonant and convincing for Eve to believe this truth. God was not holding out on her - He forbid her to eat of the fruit because He knew the consequences. God desires to protect us, and His commandments make way for the protection of our souls. But the best things are not always the things that feel good - and you and I live in a culture that shouts it like an anthem: *If it feels good, then it is good.*

Lies, once again.

One of the biggest lies that our culture feeds us as young women is the lie of what constitutes sexual freedom. Our world has reduced sex to an act you can and perhaps should do with someone on a first date - to our world, sex is neither valuable nor sacred. *The more sex you are having,* our world declares, *the more free you are.* When my husband Daniël and I were dating, we had both already decided many years prior that we wanted to give our virginity to our spouses. Our relationship was rooted in Jesus and our Catholic faith, and was built on the foundation of authentic love, which encompasses the virtue of chastity. You see, the decision to commit to chastity and abstinence in life is not one that is forever followed by smooth sailing. God is the creator of sex and He created us with sexual desires that are good - and those desires are to be carried out within the context of the Sacrament of Matrimony. Chastity is a challenging road to walk when you are in love with someone, and something you must continually talk about in order to have the strength to keep choosing it together. But God did not design sex to be a part of marriage simply because He doesn't want us to have fun or feel close to a boyfriend or fiancé. God wants you to feel close to the man you are in a relationship with - spiritually and emotionally - but He wants you to feel closest to the spouse He will guide you to if you are called to marriage. *God wants you to share the most intimate act that can take place between two people with the man who has committed his life to you.* When we look at sex in this proper context - there is no worry, hesitation, panic, regret, or sadness involved - and that, my sisters, is true freedom.

Freedom surely comes at a price. It is indeed the more challenging road, but the road which brings peace, security, and, ultimately, true and lasting fulfillment. This is the fulfillment that everyone in this life is looking for.

Choose God's road and you choose freedom. His road will always make way for the best, most fulfilling, and most beautiful things.

PRAYER

God, I trust that it gives you joy to give me the best things. I know that you set out your commandments for us to follow so that we may live in true freedom rather than be enslaved by sin. When I feel like everyone else may be having more fun, or that your commandments are hard to follow, help me to remember why a life walking with you and abiding in your ways is what will fulfill me. I trust your plan - I trust your commandments - and I trust that you know what is best for me. Most importantly, Lord, I know you want me free. Thank you for creating me for freedom. Amen.

REFLECTION

- Do you believe that God wants what is best for you? if not, what is keeping you from believing that?

- Is there an area of your life where you may have fallen for the lie of the enemy that God's laws are oppressive, and that you want to do things your own way? How does Eve's story impact your thinking about the reasoning behind God's laws?

YOU CAN'T
SIT WITH US

HANNAH AND PENINNAH

There was a certain man of Ramathaim, a Zuphite from the hill country of Ephraim, whose name was Elkanah son of Jeroham son of Elihu son of Tohu son of Zuph, an Ephraimite. He had two wives; the name of one was Hannah, and the name of the other Peninnah. Peninnah had children, but Hannah had no children.

Now this man used to go up year by year from his town to worship and to sacrifice to the Lord of hosts at Shiloh, where the two sons of Eli, Hophni and Phinehas, were priests of the Lord. On the day when Elkanah sacrificed, he would give portions to his wife Peninnah and to all her sons and daughters; but to Hannah he gave a double portion, because he loved her, though the Lord had closed her womb. Her rival used to provoke her severely, to irritate her, because the Lord had closed her womb. So it went on year after year; as often as she went up to the house of the Lord, she used to provoke her. Therefore Hannah wept and would not eat. Her husband Elkanah said to her, "Hannah, why do you weep? Why do you not eat? Why is your heart sad? Am I not more to you than ten sons?"

--1 Samuel:1-8

It strikes me every time I see the commercials for a women's boxing match or organized fight. I am always caught off guard seeing women on a commercial kicking and punching one another:

"Pay a big sum of money to buy this fight for your TV...the two top female fighters will duke it out to see who comes out on top..."

How did we ever arrive in a time when this is considered normal?

We live in a time where modern society not only condones women being unkind to one another, but considers it entertainment. We don't even need to go so far as physical fighting. Television shows often feature women that gossip about each other, hurt each other emotionally, and fight with words. Conflicts between two women are held up for entertainment. It may be odd to think there are accounts of women bullying other women in the Bible, but the story of Hannah and Peninnah is one of them.

This account occurs between the time of Judges and the reign of King David - this was an age when it was still lawful to have more than one wife. Hannah and Peninnah are both married to Elkanah, and the life they all share in is quite a predicament. Elkanah loves Hannah more than he loves Peninnah, but Peninnah is extremely fertile and able to bear children, while Hannah is barren, unable to have children at all.

Peninnah is jealous of her husband's love for Hannah, and it motivates her to provoke and bully Hannah. Scripture uses a strong adjective to describe how Peninnah provoked and irritated her - *severely*. I can only imagine the ugly words she hurled at Hannah, knowing her greatest wound of infertility and using this knowledge to cut deep into this excruciating part of Hannah's heart, forcing her to remember the unbearable reality of her barrenness time and time again. Peninnah displays the skill that women develop far too quickly to mask their own hurt - using what we know hurts our sisters to drive their pain even deeper.

Pause for a moment and consider a few examples of the glorification of women being mean to one another in our culture - the popularity of the movie *Mean Girls, The Real Housewives of Orange County* and every subsequent spinoff in Atlanta, New York, Beverly Hills, New Jersey, *The Bachelor*...turn on the television and you will see women screaming at each other, hitting each other, speaking ugly words about one another and to one another. Contemporary culture has declared this okay. Our society says this is common and acceptable behavior for women.

Contrary to our culture's belief, considering the root of who we are created to be as women - nurturing, kind, compassionate, and loving - there is nothing entertaining about women being unkind to one another. This behavior is ugly, demoralizing, and a far cry from what we are called to and, more importantly, what we were made for.

It is unlikely that you see women fighting in your day-to-day life like they do on television and in movies. However, in our everyday lives, bullying or unkindness between women is not often overt or obvious. Sometimes it comes in the form of sarcasm, little pokes and prods, jokes and snide remarks that we mask as funny or lighthearted but are directed toward a particular girl. It is unkindness all the same. Meanness comes in the form of posting comments online, spreading rumors, purposely talking about an event you know a certain girl was not invited to in front of her, or excluding another girl from a group or conversation.

Throughout my journey from my teenage years into young adulthood, I have spent time with many different women - as friends, as peers, as classmates, and as students. I have witnessed years of women being put into categories: the sporty girls, the nerds, the band geeks, the popular girls, the mean girls. I suffered from the harsh words and bullying from "mean girls" as a teenager and also walked with the girls who were bullied in the school I worked at. I have been reminded of one fact time and time again: the mean girls are often in greatest need of someone to love them. I have always come to find that beneath their mean spirit and gossiping is always a girl who is hurting and broken. Beneath the exterior of many of them is a girl who has deep and heartbreaking troubles going on at home. Beneath the tough girl facade is a young woman who simply wants to know and feel that she is accepted and loved.

When women bully each other, it always stems from the same roots - emotions and feelings of insecurity, jealousy, sadness, or competition. When these feelings come up in our hearts and minds, it can be difficult to know where to place these feelings and how to deal with them properly. When we feel bad about ourselves, it can propel us to try to bring other women down along with us.

In this account, by her cruelty to Hannah, Penninah was increasing her brokenness by bringing pain to Hannah.

Women, we must never multiply our pain. We must never allow our pain, jealousy, or insecurity to motivate us to inflict pain upon others.

It is an important question to ask ourselves: In a world full of young women who have very few kind words to say to one another, what role am I playing? Am I the woman who uplifts or the woman who tears down? Am I the one starting the gossip or stopping the gossip? Do I deal with any feelings of insecurity or jealousy properly or do I let them cause me to act out? Has there been a time in my life when a girl was being bullied, and I had the opportunity to step in and say something to stop it, and I didn't?

As daughters of God, we are called above all to love. We are called to live out compassion and empathy. We are called to be leaders who rise above this new "normal." We are called to be the women who say something when other girls are making fun of or excluding another girl. The tendency to gossip, to talk about other women behind their back, to start or spread rumors - we are called to strive for more. We are called to be the women who deal with our pain properly - by handing our hurts and our pain to God the Father. God wants to take our pains, our hurts, our brokenness through a life of intimate relationship with Him. We cannot handle the struggles of womanhood alone; He wants to walk with us and continually help us grow in grace, virtue, and holiness.

It takes tremendous courage to be the woman who rises above the rest, but in doing so, we can inspire others to do the same.

PRAYER

Lord, I know that I am called to always love my sisters in Christ. When I struggle to do so because of any feelings of competition, jealousy, insecurity, or brokenness, please help me to continually learn to love better. Help me to see every woman I encounter as my sister and as your daughter. I am sorry for the times I have been unkind or mean-spirited to other women. I ask you to heal the memories and pain I carry from when other women have been unkind, unloving, or exclusive to me. Help me live out my call as a woman to be compassionate, kind, and uplifting to all. Amen.

REFLECTION

- Do you feel a need to compete with other women? Where does that desire for competition come from? How can you change your perspective to see other women as sisters rather than competitors in life?

- Do you deal with your hurts or pain properly by turning to God? Or are you a woman who may act out like Peninnah when you are struggling?

- Is there a girl that you have been unkind to that you owe an apology to? Consider making a heartfelt apology to someone you know you have hurt with your words or actions. Is there a girl who has been mean to you that you need to forgive? Ask God to help you forgive this girl and heal you of the hurt she has caused you.

LOVE AND LIVING WATER

THE WOMAN AT THE WELL

[Jesus] had to go through Samaria. So he came to a Samaritan city called Sychar, near the plot of ground that Jacob had given to his son Joseph. Jacob's well was there, and Jesus, tired out by his journey, was sitting by the well. It was about noon.

A Samaritan woman came to draw water, and Jesus said to her, "Give me a drink." (His disciples had gone to the city to buy food.) The Samaritan woman said to him, "How is it that you, a Jew, ask a drink of me, a woman of Samaria?" (Jews do not share things in common with Samaritans.) Jesus answered her, "If you knew the gift of God, and who it is that is saying to you, 'Give me a drink,' you would have asked him, and he would have given you living water." The woman said to him, "Sir, you have no bucket, and the well is deep. Where do you get that living water? Are you greater than our ancestor Jacob, who gave us the well, and with his sons and his flocks drank from it?" Jesus said to her, " Everyone who drinks of this water will be thirsty again, but those who drink of the water that I will give them will never be thirsty. The water that I will give will become in them a spring of water gushing up to eternal life." The woman said to him, "Sir, give me this water, so that I may never be thirsty or have to keep coming here to draw water."

Jesus said to her, "Go, call your husband, and come back." The woman answered him, "I have no husband." Jesus said to her, "You are right in saying, 'I have no husband'; for you have had five husbands, and the one you have now is not your husband. What you have said is true!" The woman said to him, "Sir, I see that you are a prophet. Our ancestors worshiped on this mountain, but you say that the place where people must worship is in Jerusalem." Jesus said to her, "Woman, believe me, the hour is coming when you will worship the Father neither on this mountain nor in Jerusalem. You worship what you do not know; we worship what we know, for salvation is from the Jews. But the hour is coming, and is now here, when the true worshipers will worship the Father in spirit and truth, for the Father seeks such as these to worship him. God is spirit, and those who worship him must worship in spirit and truth." The woman said to him, "I know that Messiah is coming" (who is called Christ). "When he comes, he will proclaim all things to us." Jesus said to her, "I am he, the one who is speaking to you."

Just then his disciples came. They were astonished that he was speaking with a woman, but no one said, "What do you want?" or, "Why are you speaking with her?" Then the woman left her water-jar and went back to the city. She said to the people, "Come and see a man who told me everything I have ever done! He cannot be the Messiah, can he?" They left the city and were on their way to him.

Many Samaritans from that city believed in him because of the woman's testimony, "He told me everything I have ever done." So when the Samaritans came to him, they asked him to stay with them; and he stayed there for two days. And many more believed because of his word. They said to the woman, "It is no longer because of what you said that we believe, for we have heard for ourselves, and we know that this is truly the Savior of the world."

--John 4: 1-30, 39-42

Five husbands. Man #6.

The thought of going through five husbands is unbelievable to many women. But these figures make it apparent that throughout her life, the woman at the well was constantly trying to fill the void in her heart with the love of a man.

It is apparent throughout her encounter with Jesus that she is hungry for something. She is longing for fulfillment. She desires true, deep, and authentic love.

And she looks for it in men.

It is a story of womanhood told throughout the ages - women deeply desiring the love of a man, experiencing the desires to be protected, to be held, to be admired, and to be treasured unconditionally.

As women, we were born with a natural tendency to desire attention and affirmation from the opposite sex. The Samaritan woman was living out this desire and Jesus knew it. There is no record of whether her husbands were dying, leaving, or divorcing her, but Jesus knows of her past and speaks it out loud into the air between them.

Maybe you remember a time when you were like this woman - a time when you would have loved for a man to pay attention to you, to affirm you, to fill you up with love. Perhaps you are experiencing that

in this very moment in your life. I have certainly experienced those times. I first felt this tendency in high school. I wanted to be asked to the homecoming dance; both my sisters went nearly every year. I, on the other hand, was not asked a single time. It was disappointing. I wanted boys to talk to me at school dances or at football games and it was a monumental occasion when girls received their first kiss. As high school progressed, I remained in the "never been kissed club." Friends would excitedly hop in the car as we drove to school on Monday morning and shriek about how they got their first kiss over the weekend after the football game or on a date. Every girl seemed to be talking to some guy and I started to wonder and feel left out...is there something wrong with me? Am I not desirable or attractive enough? Is it normal to go through high school without ever having kissed a boy? I had bought into the lie our society feeds us that relationships are the one thing that makes a person happier. I had bought into the lie that if guys are not paying attention, I must be less beautiful. I had fallen into the trap of thinking that what a guy does or does not think about me plays a part in who I am. It doesn't. Your relationship status and whatever some boy thinks or does not think about you says nothing about *who you are*.

In our makeup as women, we are born with inherent desires to feel safe, cared for, sought-after, and beautiful. We want to be paid attention to by the guy we like or to have him respond to our existence in some way, shape, or form. We want physical affection. We want to feel protected. We desire affirmation. We want to be told and to know that we are valued. These desires and feelings are all normal; there is nothing wrong or bad about our want to be affirmed and accepted by men. *The important factor is the way we direct this desire in our hearts and in our actions.*

Some women pour everything they have into a search for a boyfriend, trying to fill this desire in every worldly way. They respond to this hunger by spending much of their time running from crush to crush, boyfriend to boyfriend, in hopes of finding fulfillment and love, in hopes that being with the physical body of a man will make them feel complete or whole or accepted. Some women give their bodies to men they have known for only a few days or hours. Some women have sex with a man in hopes that he will call the next day and her fairy tale will begin, even when they know deep in their hearts that it never works that way. Other women are terrified of being alone. They cannot be without a boyfriend. They do not feel they can exist without a guy to call, to text, to lean on, to hang out with. They jump from relationship to relationship because this craving for affirmation has taken over their heart and life. They are too scared of what their life would look like without the attention of another.

Maybe the woman at the well is reflective of one of your friends, or a woman in your high school or college

or group of friends. Maybe the woman at the well was you in your past. Maybe she is reflective of you in this very moment.

This pursuit of a man's love leaves many of us feeling bruised, broken, and emptier than we were before the search began. Too many women live with painful, deep, and lasting regret at all they have given away to men who did not deserve it. I know that pain. I have sisters who know that pain. It digs in deep and leaves wounds that, if we do not let Jesus place His healing hand on them, can last forever.

The woman at the well is experiencing this pain. When Jesus speaks her pain aloud she quickly changes the subject. Which one of us wouldn't when the person sitting next to us brings up our deepest wounds and sin? Jesus knows she is as empty as the jar she brought to the well that day; Her heart was scarred by failed relationships and a lack of authentic, deep fulfillment. The "water" she was filling herself with evaporated into thin air - it was water that did not suffice in her extreme spiritual dehydration.

And, as Jesus always does, he gently and lovingly teaches her where to direct her desires - to the water that gives life.

He teaches her with love and peace...*Direct these desires in your heart to me and you will find true and lasting fulfillment.*

He wants you and I both to know this deep in our minds and hearts: No man He has created is going to satisfy our hunger. No man on earth can make us feel as affirmed and loved as He can. No one man on earth can speak beauty into our hearts the same way He does. No boyfriend, no fiancé, no husband can do for us what Jesus wants to do for us.

He created us to find love in Him - to find our hearts full in Him - to let Him be the first one who says, "You are mine. You are valued. You are loved."

Jesus reveals His unending love to the woman at the well in this encounter, and upon receiving this truth - she leaves her water jar behind. She leaves it behind because she now knows what will quench her parched heart. She now knows of the water that will sustain her and bring meaning and authentic love to her life.

She is not the same.

She knows where her hunger for love can be met - in a true, authentic, and deep relationship of intimacy and love with the Savior of all the world. This relationship with the Savior is available to you right now on this very day.

Are you ready and willing to leave your water jar at the well and be filled up by the love of our King?

PRAYER

God, I have these desires to be loved, to be paid attention to, to be recognized as beautiful. You have placed these desires for relationship within me - I ask that you help me place my desires to love you first in my life. When I get discouraged because it seems like everyone else is happy - help me to be encouraged that you love me with a more fierce love than any man on earth could provide for me. I know you are always pursuing me, Lord, and I accept your pursuit. You are my all in all, may my desire for a relationship with a man never trump my desire for a relationship with you. Amen.

REFLECTION

- Do you find yourself to be like the woman at the well? What can you learn from her experience with Jesus Christ and the truth that He offers the same water of life to you?

- Were you the woman at the well in your past? How did God bring you out of that season of your life? Reflect on the way God pursued you through your desires for a man's love.

GIVING BEYOND MEASURE

THE WIDOW WITH
TWO COINS

He sat down opposite the treasury, and watched the crowd putting money into the treasury. Many rich people put in large sums. A poor widow came and put in two small copper coins, which are worth a penny. Then he called his disciples and said to them, "Truly I tell you, this poor widow has put in more than all those who are contributing to the treasury. For all of them have contributed out of their abundance; but she out of her poverty has put in everything she had, all she had to live on."

--Mark 12:41-44

What if the Lord stops providing for me? What if I cannot afford to pay my bills? What if I do not have enough money to buy the things I like or want?

I imagine that no such question crossed the widow's mind. She would not have given everything she had if she was occupied with worry about these things.

Many times people focus on financial giving upon looking at this widow's account in the Gospel. We use this account as a means to teach people about tithing and giving to the Church. Certainly, Jesus highlights her example of true and generous giving in the midst of people giving financially. However, Christ presents each and every one of us with an individual call to live generously, and that call looks different for each one of us at different stages in our lives. For some of us that means monetary generosity, for others generosity of the heart. For some it means generosity with our lives...whatever this call is, Christ wants our response and our giving to look like hers.

This woman does not give in expectation. She gives in trust.

I met two young women in the summer of 2013 at two different Life Teen camps. They are both wonderful American girls, born and raised in a land of opportunity, privilege, and first world problems. Sometime during their college experience, God placed within their hearts a call to radical generosity.

Both of them seized the opportunity to respond to this call. They did not respond to God's invitation with money - they responded to His call with their lives and became missionaries when God asked them to move to Haiti. They welcomed the opportunity to move to a new land, to live with the poor and serve the poor. They learned a new language, and continually strive to be God's hands and feet in a country that desperately needs to encounter the living God. In their day to day life, they work with children, teens, and adults alike. They minister day in and day out, living in the normal Haitian conditions with bugs and wildlife - a lifestyle that would make most Americans very uncomfortable. They are living the example of this woman - giving their all to God in a response of complete and unwavering trust in His goodness. In this case, God did not want their money - he wanted their whole self - even if just for a few years. There is no material gain in return for the gift of their hearts to the Haitian people,yet they give all they have with great joy and great love.

You certainly do not have to move to Haiti in order to give sacrificially. There are many avenues through which you can give beyond measure. I have a friend who works a job at a local clothing store. She does not make a lot of money, but she has decided to set aside a certain percentage of her paycheck every month to donate to a new charity. This allows her the opportunity to research many different charities to see the ways people are giving and support many different organizations doing great things for people. Another woman I know spends a great deal of her free time volunteering at soup kitchens for the homeless. She goes there on Saturdays and during school breaks to give of her time to a ministry that really needs as many people helping as possible. There are countless ways to give, and it is important for each one of us to consider what we are most passionate about and how we can give of our time, talent, or treasure to that group of people, ministry, or organization.

Ultimately, God does not need our things or our money. He simply wants our hearts to be brimming with generosity and the willingness to sacrifice. A life in Christ is always a life of generosity, but our worries about His provision keep us from believing His promise that He will provide. I meet many young people who experience fear in giving what God is asking them to give or go where God is calling them to go. In our humanity, we worry that if we jump at His call He will not be there on the other end. We worry that when He calls us to massive generosity He will not take care of us. God will never call you to generosity and then disappear. God will always follow through.

But what if there is an exception to that "always"? God wants us to put away our "what ifs" when He calls us to great obedience and sacrifice. Our "what ifs" come from disbelief in God's faithfulness and a lack of faith in His promises. Imagine all the people who could have let "what ifs" keep them from responding in great generosity to God's call. Worry could have kept Joan of Arc at home rather than in battle, many martyrs from witnessing to their faith and dying for the cause of Christ, many priests from entering into their vocation, and Mary from answering an obedient, "yes," to the message of the angel Gabriel.

He wants us all to live a resounding, "yes" - a "fiat" to His call.

God will call you to generosity and will outdo your generosity. He did it for all the named and unnamed saints and has done it for millions of others. In highlighting this woman's giving of her two coins, we know He will care for her as He cares for us. We know that He sees what she gives in the same way He sees what we give.

Be generous with God as this widow was and He will be generous with you. God's return for our generosity does not often look like a full bank account. His generosity most often looks like richness in His love, the richness of wonderful friends and community, or the richness of peace and lasting joy.

This joy is priceless, and the widow knew it well.

PRAYER

Lord, I know you call me to give generously in my life - I ask that you give me the grace to be like the widow who gives her last two coins. I pray for a heart brimming with generosity and a willingness to give sacrificially - from my heart, from my life, from my gifts, or from my bank account. I trust that you will always provide for me. I trust that you will always come through. Help me to trust you ever more. Amen.

REFLECTION

- What are the two coins in your life that you feel you can't give up or let go of? How can the widow's example encourage you to entrust these things to God?

- Is there something in your life you feel God is calling you to give that will extend you - your time, your money, your life? Do you trust that if you give that, that He will respond to your obedience?

BRAZEN

ESTHER

Therefore we have decreed that those indicated to you in the letters written by Haman, who is in charge of affairs and is our second father, shall all - wives and children included - be utterly destroyed by the swords of their enemies, without pity or restraint, on the fourteenth day of the twelfth month.

When Esther's maids and her eunuchs came and told her, the queen was deeply distressed; she sent garments to clothe Mordecai, so that he might take off his sackcloth; but he would not accept them. Then Esther called for Hathach, one of the king's eunuchs, who had been appointed to attend her, and ordered him to go to Mordecai to learn what was happening and why. Hathach went out to Mordecai in the open square of the city in front of the king's gate, and Mordecai told him all that had happened to him, and the exact sum of money that Haman had promised to pay into the king's treasuries for the destruction of the Jews. Mordecai also gave him a copy of the written decree issued in Susa for their destruction, that he might show it to Esther, explain it to her, and charge her to go to the king to make supplication to him and entreat him for her people.

Hatach went and told Esther what Mordecai had said. Then Esther spoke to Hatach and gave him a message for Mordecai saying, "All the king's servants and the people of the king's provinces know that if any man or woman goes to the king inside the inner court without being called, there is but one law - all alike are to be put to death. Only if the king holds out the golden sceptre to someone, may that person live. I myself have not been called to come in to the king for thirty days." When they told Mordecai what Esther had said, Mordecai told them to reply to Esther, "Do not think that in the king's palace you will escape any more than all the other Jews. For if you keep silence at such a time as this, relief and deliverance will rise for the Jews from another quarter, but you and your father's family will perish. Who knows? Perhaps you have *come to royal dignity for just such a time as this." Then Esther said in reply to Mordecai, "Go, gather all the Jews to be found in Susa, and hold a fast on my behalf, and neither eat nor drink for three days, night or day. I and my maids will also fast as you do. After that I will go to the king, though it is against the law; and if I perish, I perish."*

--Esther 3:6; 4: 1-16

When I reflect on the lives of the martyrs of our Church, I often ask myself... If I am ever faced with the opportunity to die for what I know is right, will I have the courage to do so?

The account of Esther's life is very long and involved. In summary, the queen steps down because she refuses to be ogled at by the drunk king and his friends, and a beauty pageant of sorts is held for the king to pick a new queen out of a select group of women. Esther is chosen and becomes queen, unbeknownst to the king that she is Jewish - this must be kept a secret. Her cousin Mordecai, who raised her and works within the king's courts, finds out that one of the king's associates has put out a decree to have all the Jews in their city exterminated. Esther learns of this decree, and knows that as queen, she alone holds the responsibility of making sure her people are not wiped out entirely. During the time of this king's reign, a person risked death for approaching the king without being summoned, but approaching him is the only hope Esther has at convincing the king to reverse this declaration. She approaches the king with an unwavering courage in doing what she knows she must do. The king accepts her request, and the Jews are saved because Esther steps up in brazen boldness. They are all saved because she does what she knows is right.

She did what she had to do - even in the face of death. Esther was *bold*. She was fearless. She was steadfast. And boldness is a crucial characteristic of someone who wishes to follow God with absolute and unwavering faithfulness.

Esther's story can be difficult to grasp in light of our own lives. She was a queen during a time when a king could murder anyone he was displeased with at a moment's notice. But her boldness burned like a fire within her and has caused her story to be told and read for thousands of years.

Her fearlessness brings to mind one of the martyrs who inspires me most from the 20th century - José Sánchez del Río.

Blessed José Sánchez del Río is a beatified martyr in our Church who was part of the Cristero War in Mexico in the early 1900s. The Mexican government made a disturbing movement to eliminate the Catholic Church in Mexico and began to seize churches, close Catholic schools, and even execute Catholic priests. Young José was part of the uprising against the government, and their battle cry was "Viva Cristo Rey!" which translates to "Long Live Christ the King." At a young age, Jose was allowed to join the rebel forces against the government. In one battle, he was captured by the government forces and imprisoned in a Catholic Church.

The government militia did everything they could to get José to renounce his faith. He refused.
Viva Cristo Rey, he would say over and over again in the midst of torture and impending death.

In the face of death, he did what he had to do. He did what he knew was right.

Esther says it with great conviction, *"If I perish, I perish."*

Jose echoes this level of boldness.

The soldiers skinned his feet and made him walk on the dirty road. Jose screamed in pain and the soldiers gave him a way out - just say *Death to Christ the King.*

"I will never give in. Viva Cristo Rey."

He died a martyr at fourteen.

These two, Esther and José, looked death square in the eye, and refused to back down in their mission. One lived, the other did not, but they were each willing to lay down their life for what they knew was right.

I have never had to be bold in the face of death. It is likely that you have not, either. But are we bold in carrying out what we know is right? Sometimes I wonder about us, as young Catholics, if we are consistently willing to do what is right - *even in the face of embarrassment.*
Have you ever been embarrassed to tell your friends that you just got back from retreat? Ever been too embarrassed to say you had to leave an event, miss practice, or miss something entirely because you had to attend Mass? Ever been too ashamed to tell your friends you can't go out with them to see that new movie because of the content of it? Have you ever felt too awkward to tell the guy you are dating that you are saving sex for marriage?

We are called be bold in testifying to all that is encompassed in our faith - the sacraments we partake in, the morals and values we uphold, the things in the world we just will not and cannot participate in. Our Catholic faith is not the norm. In our society going to Mass is abnormal. Saving sex for marriage is abnormal. Choosing not to watch movies filled with sexual filth, crudeness, and bad language is very uncommon. So we get embarrassed and feel awkward. We are not so bold in saying, "Sorry, I can't go to see that movie. No, I will not go to the party. Yes, I am saving my virginity for my future husband."

Why? Why is it so hard to say these things out loud? How can we live embarrassed about what we believe when José was ready and willing to die for what he believed?

Where is Esther's boldness within us?

It is a boldness that we must find within ourselves, and a boldness that I have been able to find within myself by the grace of God. It is the boldness that helped me to tell a few college friends on a long-awaited girl's weekend trip once, "Tomorrow's Sunday, so I need to find a church close by where I can get to Mass. Any of you are more than welcome to come with me." It is the fearlessness that helped me decline every invitation to come out to the big parties at Arizona State University, or caused me to stay home during the University "Undie

Run" (which has a self-explanatory title) that many people asked me to join in on. The opportunities to be bold in our faith come in all different shapes and sizes; they are all no less an invitation to courageously live what we believe.

Esther declared, "If I perish, I perish." I want you to remember her words. I want you to remember them deep in your soul - because while it is unlikely you will look death in the face, you will look laughter and persecution and peer pressure in the face if you stand for what is good and right in this world... and I want your response to echo hers... *If they laugh, they laugh. If he breaks up with me for my values, He breaks up with me. If they call me names, they call me names. If they ask why I can't go, I will tell them why I can't go. I will stand up - strong and fearless - no matter what.*

Let boldness push you on. May the boldness of Esther carry you forward. May the boldness of faith cause you to speak up and live as a countercultural witness to a life in the heart of an unwavering and all-powerful God. *Viva Cristo Rey.*

PRAYER

God, I humbly ask that you give me the boldness of Esther to live out my faith and to choose what is right. Sometimes it is incredibly difficult to do what I know is right - especially in the face of embarrassment and peer pressure. I ask that you make me a brave witness to truth, and that you awaken within me the courage to choose to stand for you in every moment I feel like staying silent or going with the flow of the world around me. Amen.

REFLECTION

- Do you feel that you are a woman who consistently chooses what is right? What is helping on this path - your friends, your family, a consistent prayer life? If not, what is keeping you from being able to consistently do the right thing?

- How vocal are you in your life about what you believe - by your actions and words? Do you go with the flow of what everyone else seems to be doing or are you confident in standing up for your values? What changes do you need to make in order to help you stand strong in the face of embarrassment?

- Is there a woman in your life who you admire for the way she boldly lives her faith? What is it that you admire most about her bravery and how do you let her example impact the way you live out your faith?

THE BOLD EVANGELIST

PRISCILLA

After this Paul left Athens and went to Corinth. There he found a Jew named Aquila, a native of Pontus, who had recently come from Italy with his wife Priscilla, because Claudius had ordered all Jews to leave Rome. Paul went to see them, and, because he was of the same trade, he stayed with them, and they worked together -- by trade they were tentmakers. Every sabbath he would argue in the synagogue and would try to convince Jews and Greeks.

After staying there for a considerable time, Paul said farewell to the believers and sailed for Syria, accompanied by Priscilla and Aquila.

Now there came to Ephesus a Jew named Apollos, a native of Alexandria. He was an eloquent man, well-versed in the scriptures. He had been instructed in the way of the Lord; and he spoke with burning enthusiasm and taught accurately the things concerning Jesus, though he knew only the baptism of John. He began to speak boldly in the synagogue; but when Priscilla and Aquila heard him, they took him aside and explained the Way of God to him more accurately. And when he wished to cross over to Achaia, the believers encouraged him and wrote to the disciples to welcome him. On his arrival he greatly helped those who through grace had become believers, for he powerfully refuted the Jews in public, showing by the Scriptures that the Messiah is Jesus.

--Acts 18:1-4, 18, 24-28

It is easy to take a back seat when there is someone else willing to do all the evangelizing. Evangelization is an important mission given to us by Christ himself; it is the mission to bring the Good News of salvation into every situation and to help bring others to believe in and know Jesus Christ and His saving power. Evangelization is twofold; it involves both the witness of living an authentic faith and spreading the truth of the Gospel in concrete ways.

I have often thought of my role in evangelization in terms of seats in a car. What seat are you sitting in? The driver's seat? The passenger seat? The back seat? Maybe you are tied to the back as someone pulls you along behind?

Once she knew the truth about Jesus Christ and salvation, Priscilla took the driver's seat and never looked back. We first encounter her in the Acts of the Apostles when Paul meets her and her husband, and they embark on a journey of incredible friendship and companionship.

There is one thing apparent from the start - Priscilla takes her role in spreading the Good News of Christ's life, death, and Resurrection very seriously. Teaching others the truth of the Messiah is of paramount importance in her life and her marriage to Aquila. Priscilla and Aquila become missionaries of the Word as they travel with Paul to continue to spread the truth about the life of Jesus Christ. When it comes time to move and reach more people, she goes.

Priscilla does not fear moving into the unknown to carry the Good News. She is a diligent learner of the Word and stays close to Paul in order to keep learning all that she can. Priscilla shows us what it means to follow Christ courageously and to maintain a hunger to grow in faith. Priscilla demonstrates what it means to be a fearless female evangelist and leader.

This bold woman did not wait around for other people to champion the movement of evangelization in her community. She took it upon herself to make sure everyone in proximity knew the Good News of the Passion of Jesus Christ and the salvation offered to each of them. It mentions a few times in Scripture that she gathered people to hold church in her home, counseled others, and traveled to where the truth needed to be taken.

She seized her great role as evangelist. She did not leave it to someone else.

When you get involved in your youth group or college ministry, you will encounter many peers who are great leaders. There are people who are running every kind of Catholic club, music ministry, and retreat team. When we are surrounded by people like this, sometimes our human tendency to sit back and relax starts to creep in. We think:

There isn't a role for me. Everyone's already taken all the jobs. Melissa is way more qualified for that than

I am. I wouldn't know where to begin. I don't have the leadership skills that Sophia has. I'm not cut out to be a leader in the Church.

There will always be a role for you when it comes to bringing people to know Christ. *A life of faith is a life of action.*

Some people mistakenly believe that evangelization solely involves preaching or some form of public ministry or leadership position. There are individuals under the impression that you must have some prominent role as a Catholic speaker, retreat leader, musician, or campus ministry president to be able to evangelize. However, the Scriptural accounts make no mention of Priscilla ever speaking in the streets or into a microphone. She evangelized by holding church in her home. She brought people to the fullness of truth by one-on-one conversation. She led people by walking with them. That is the sign of an incredible evangelist... the one who is willing to journey with people. We can see this through her personal encounter with Apollos and teaching him the truth of Jesus when she sees that he needs help and direction. She invests her time and energy into walking with him, and he is later referenced as a great evangelizer of the time, helping many others to come to know Christ.

In our day to day lives, evangelization begins in the smallest of scales. Evangelization begins by investing in others and caring for their souls. Be hospitable. Share your testimony of faith if an opportunity arises. Invite someone to church. Talk about your faith lovingly with your family members who may not care about faith at all. Be courageous in witnessing to counter-cultural decisions of modesty and chastity. Post faith-related things on social media. Be accessible to people. Say grace before meals. Take a role in the parish - lector, be a Eucharistic minister, or usher. There are countless ways to simply love people, and in loving them help them to see that your love comes from God.

It is easy to give into complacency when we are surrounded by the spiritual go-getters. It is easy to skate through and let other people plan retreats, women's groups, or start Bible studies, or share their testimony at school or invite someone to church. It is easy to let other people do the work of sharing the Gospel while we navigate and enjoy our own little personal walk with Jesus.

Women, we are called to be bold evangelizers. We are called to be courageous champions of truth.

There is an urgency for the Gospel in the time we live in, and you have what it takes to share the Gospel with everyone who crosses the path of your life. Follow Priscilla's lead. There is no time for sitting back; Christ is calling us to take the front seat and bring a message of hope, love, and redemption to the masses.

PRAYER

Lord, I ask that you give me a heart for evangelizing my family, my friends, my community, and the world. Help me to live a life of action and find the role I have to play in spreading the Good News of your life, death, and Resurrection with the people who need to hear it most. When I feel like I don't have a place or a job, allow me to see how I can walk with people, one-on-one, toward understanding who you are. I want to offer the gifts I have to bringing people to you - help me to realize my gifts and use them for the Kingdom. Amen.

REFLECTION

- What seat are you occupying in the car of evangelization? Do you take your role of sharing your faith seriously, or do you leave it to other people?

- Think of someone in your life who evangelizes in a way that you admire. What is it about the way they share God's love that you admire? How can you emulate what you admire about them in your own life?

ARISE

JAIRUS' DAUGHTER

When Jesus had crossed again in the boat to the other side, a great crowd gathered round him; and he was by the lake. Then one of the leaders of the synagogue named Jairus came and, when he saw him, fell at his feet and begged him repeatedly, "My little daughter is at the point of death. Come and lay your hands on her, so that she may be made well, and live." So he went with him.

While he was still speaking, some people came from the leader's house to say, "Your daughter is dead. Why trouble the teacher any further?" But overhearing what they said, Jesus said to the leader of the synagogue, "Do not fear, only believe." He allowed no one to follow him except Peter, James, and John, the brother of James. When they came to the house of the leader of the synagogue, he saw a commotion, people weeping and wailing loudly. When he had entered, he said to them, "Why do you make a commotion and weep? The child is not dead but sleeping." And they laughed at him. Then he put them all outside, and took the child's father and mother and those who were with him, and went in where the child was. He took her by the hand and said to her, "Talitha cum," which means, "Little girl, get up!" And immediately the girl got up and began to walk about (she was twelve years of age). At this they were overcome with amazement. He strictly ordered them that no one should know this, and told them to give her something to eat.

--Mark 5:21-24, 35-43

Sometimes I ponder what it must have been like for St. Joan of Arc to hear that first call from God. Saint Joan was born a peasant girl, and while working in her family's garden when she was just 13 years old, Sts. Michael, Catherine, and Margaret appeared to her in visions. She had been hearing their voices in prayer intermittently throughout her life, but this vision was different. Each of these saints told her that she must drive the English from the French territory, and bring the Dauphin to the French city of Reims for his coronation... a totally unthinkable feat, even for a skilled military man.

Can you imagine how utterly bewildered this young girl must have been? Three saints asking her to lead a military movement for the Lord at the age of *thirteen?* This was her moment when the Lord spoke clearly into her soul just as he spoke to Jairus' daughter... "Little girl, I say to you, arise." God chooses little Joan and when she rises to her occasion of bravery for the cause of Christ, she changes the course of the history of her country.

In the same way that He commanded Jairus' daughter, in the same way that He placed His unmistakable call on the life of young Joan, God calls us women to rise.

This rising to which we are called is not so much of a standing but a surrender. Our rising begins by declaring to God our understanding that we were created to be in relationship with Him and to love Him. It begins with the admission that we know in our hearts that we belong to no one but Him.

Do you know that deep down in your soul? You belong to the living God and he has an earth-shaking plan for your life. *He calls you to rise and see what power can unfold when you surrender to this truth.*

There is a stunning mosaic in the back of the Sacré Coeur Basilica in Paris, France. It is called *The Mosaic of Christ in Glory.* This massive mosaic depicts Jesus in a white robe, arms outstretched in triumph, with a Sacred Heart of gold in the middle of His chest. He is surrounded by dozens of saints and various depictions of important moments of Church history in France. I visited Paris for the first time in 2013, and when I first gazed on this mosaic, I looked carefully at many of the people depicted. I looked for a while at each person illustrated, and then my eyes came upon the feet of Christ. Right there, in the place closest to our Lord, is St. Joan of Arc. She is kneeling, in full armor with her sword at her side, and her arms are outstretched in a symbol of total surrender.

Here I am, Lord. My life is yours. Send me.

While I was in the Sacré Coeur, I knelt for a while, and I could not take my eyes off of her. *She is showing me how to live.*

"Although I would have rather remained spinning wool at my mother's side," Joan is quoted as saying, "I must go and do this, for my Lord wills that I do so." Surrender. Obedience. Rising.

Jesus called out to Jairus' daughter in one moment, but in our lives He is always calling. We get to decide each day if we will live our lives like Joan - with arms stretched out to the Father, surrendered to His will, placing our lives in His hands, saying, *"Here I am. Send me."* It is a monumental recognition, knowing in the depths of my soul that God's plans are better than my plans and what He wants for my life is far more magnificent than what I hope for in my life. *Handing it all over to Him is the one way to really live.*

He has called many women over the course of the existence of the universe to surrender in obedience to His call to rise. Mary, his mother. Saint Joan of Arc, indeed. Saint Agatha, St. Dymphna, St. Bernadette, St. Catherine, Blessed Chiara Luce - all the named and unnamed saints - the women, wives, mothers, daughters, sisters who were called to live a life dedicated to the cause of Christ. We walk step by step with these valiant women who answered God's summons in their life. *Little girl, I say to you, arise.*

Each of their callings to surrender were unique to their soul. A calling to rise was not always a call to a sword and battle like it was for St. Joan, but for some a calling to rise was the call to suffer with dignity and grace. For some their rising was the surrender in laying down their life plans and accepting God's will - the obedience to heed God's promptings and enter the convent in a life of total service and dedication as Christ's spouse. For some the response to their calling came in laying down their life for a husband, for children, for a family - for others their obedience to God's call placed them in the ranks of the heroic female martyrs of our Catholic Church.

Jairus' daughter responds to the call of Christ; she heeds His call and what happens to her? She comes alive. *Living in response to God's call brings a soul to life.*

Too often, our first response is to remind God of how little, how incapable, how scared we feel. We say, "Ok, God. Here are the parts of me I think maybe you could use. The other parts of my life are not much good for anything." We squirm and we attempt to reason with God and we put our finger on our chest, pointing to our frail selves and declare in astonishment, "Me, really? Lord, you must mean someone else. Not now, just wait a little while and call me again when I feel more ready. Call someone more qualified. *I am afraid.*"

That's the thing about fear - it stands in opposition to trust in a loving God. In our obedience God wants to speak into our quaking hearts again and again, "*Do not fear. Only believe.*"

Joan would have rather stayed in the comfort of home, spinning wool. She did not feel ready. And yet she rose.

If you choose to rise, you will be called to hard and magnificent things. Your rising will be a refusal of the comforts the world offers. Your rising will be a commitment to a counter-cultural life of saying, "Yes," to the things that make you free and, "No," to the things that enslave. Your rising will cause you to move, to go, to sing, to cry, and to keep forging ahead in what you know is good and true... the power of Jesus Christ and His hand on your life. This call to rise will happen many times in your walk with Christ. He will call you to new things in new seasons and ask you to walk down different pathways as the years go on. We do not rise to the occasion of God's call once; a life of faith invites us to do it time and time again.

The courage which rising requires will never come from you, my sister. It will come from the God who dwells within you. He is the same God who dwelt within Jairus' daughter and Joan, the same God who healed lepers, who put up His hand to calm a storm, who loved the lost, who fashioned the universe far beyond the limits our human minds will ever fathom.

That God, our God, has chosen you, His daughter.

You have an irreplaceable, unrepeatable role to play in God's Kingdom.

Will you take heart and rise?

PRAYER

Here I am, Lord. My life is yours. Send me.

REFLECTION

- Has there ever been a time in your life you have heard Jesus call out to you, "Little girl, I say to you, arise"? How did you respond? Did anything hold you back from responding? What was it that held you back?

- Surrender. Obedience. Rising. What are some of the ways you can concretely live out each of these words in your life?

- Take some time as you finish up this book to really reflect on the last few paragraphs of this chapter. How do you hear God calling you, right here and right now, to respond in bravery to His love?

YOUR STORY

The stories of these women will continue to be carried on through Scripture as long as the world is in motion. The next chapter belongs to you. Your life is the next great story that God is writing in this very moment. You are His daughter, He has His hand on your life and gives you all the power necessary to carry out His great plan.

As I said in Priscilla's story, a life of faith is a life of action. I pray that these stories can propel you to seek God's heart as a young woman in the middle of a restless and troubled world. I hope their stories stir and awaken within you a desire for a life of deeper prayer and meaning. I have told you many times throughout these pages - a life handed over to God is beautifully challenging but magnificently worthwhile. You are not alone on your walk - you walk with the saints and the women of Scripture. You walk with the faithful and courageous women who surround you. We are the women of the Church... and the Church is in need of our hearts, in need of our voices, and in need of our love.

Lastly, I want you to know I believe in you. I believe that you can live a life of magnificent and awe-inspiring faith and virtue. I know that you hold the possibilities within you of creating incredible change in the world and that your love and your passion for the lost and the needy can bring souls desperate for love to life. I believe that you can stand up for what is good and true even when it hurts - that you can choose good things for yourself and your heart over and over again. I believe that in seasons of pain and heartbreak you have the bravery within you to choose God - the answer that will always bring real healing. I know that you can be a friend of steadfast loyalty and that you can be a woman who places God first in everything, in every season and every year of your life. I believe that you can give selflessly beyond your wildest imaginations and that you can be a woman of power who shows every woman you encounter in your lifetime just how wonderful the great adventure of loving God can be. I am cheering you on, my sister. God is walking with you every step of the way.

I am praying for you.

Let's choose the sky.

LIFE TEEN

Leading Teens Closer to Christ
www.LifeTeen.com